**Why You
Why Me
Why Now**

Why You
Why Me
Why Now

*The Mindset and Moves
to Land That First Job,
from Networking to
Cover Letters, Resumes,
and Interviews*

RACHEL TOOR

The University of Chicago Press
Chicago and London

The University of Chicago Press, Chicago 60637
The University of Chicago Press, Ltd., London
© 2024 by Rachel Toor
Published 2024
Printed in the United States of America

33 32 31 30 29 28 27 26 25 24   1 2 3 4 5

ISBN-13: 978-0-226-83114-5 (cloth)
ISBN-13: 978-0-226-82229-7 (paper)
ISBN-13: 978-0-226-83113-8 (e-book)
DOI: https://doi.org/10.7208/chicago/9780226831138.001.0001

Library of Congress Cataloging-in-Publication Data
Names: Toor, Rachel, author.
Title: Why you, why me, why now : the mindset and moves to land that first job,
    from networking to cover letters, resumes, and interviews / Rachel Toor.
Description: Chicago : The University of Chicago Press, 2024. | Includes
    bibliographical references and index.
Identifiers: LCCN 2023036227 | ISBN 9780226831145 (cloth) | ISBN
    9780226822297 (paperback) | ISBN 9780226831138 (ebook)
Subjects: LCSH: Applications for positions. | Résumés (Employment) |
    Employment interviewing. | Job hunting. | Business writing—Technique.
Classification: LCC HF5383 .T664 2024 | DDC 650.14/2—dc23/eng/20230823
LC record available at https://lccn.loc.gov/2023036227

♾ This paper meets the requirements of ANSI/NISO Z39.48-1992
(Permanence of Paper).

Contents

Before We Begin: Why Me vii

Introduction 1

1 Attitude 17

2 The Search 27

3 The Job Description 55

4 A Few Words about "Match" 78

5 The Cover Letter 85

6 The Resume 112

7 The Interview 129

8 References 168

9 Following Up 174

10 The Long (Long, Long) Haul 180

One Last Thing: My Little Bag of Writing Tricks 187

Acknowledgments 199

Index 203

Before We Begin: Why Me

When my students want me to serve as a job reference, I ask them to show me their cover letters and resumes.

These documents often make me want to weep.

On the page, the intelligent, creative, and talented people I know come off as cocky, self-centered, and just plain unlikable. How can that be?

When it comes to applying for jobs, my students seem to forget everything I've taught them. So I remind them to use the skills they've learned in my creative writing courses to sound more like themselves, to be conversational,* and to rely on old-fashioned storytelling in their application materials. I repeat what I say in class: If you can craft a clear, concise, authentic narrative that shows the best, most vulnerable version of yourself in a way that engages the reader, you'll have the keys to the kingdom. I assure them—often first-gen college students whose parents worried they were wasting time and money studying creative writing— that what they learned in my classes is the most important skill set they could have acquired in college, no matter what profession they want to pursue.†

---

*Good writing rarely relies on fancy, multisyllabic words. Being conversational on the page is a way to let your personality shine through your prose. Even in "professional" contexts, you want to sound like a human, not a machine.

†All professors believe that what they teach is the most important subject. I'm actually right.

My goal in this book is to teach you some of those same transferable moves and tricks and to nurture a mindset that will assist you in nabbing a first "real" job.*

Applying for jobs now is both easier and harder than it's ever been. Everyone has access to an abundance of information about industries, careers, organizations, friends, strangers—and, with a few clicks, the ability to find embarrassing photos and ill-considered social media rants.

For some time, large organizations have used artificial intelligence "bots" to screen application materials. I will help you tailor what you submit so you won't be automatically rejected. But the role of AI keeps expanding. AI software can now write your cover letters for you. That may seem like a good idea, and in fact, with a well-crafted prompt, could be useful in generating first drafts. But you will still need to work hard to make sure the prose sounds like you—the person who will show up for an interview.

You can be in direct contact with those far outside your personal circle by connecting on LinkedIn or sliding into their DMs. But that doesn't mean everyone will respond. When I read my students' cover letters, I cringe at the sterile, generic prose that disguises the lovely, quirky people I know. It's like they've put on an older relative's uncomfortable suit that reeks of cigars and musty cologne. I also see lots of avoidable mistakes. Based on their application materials, I can't imagine why anyone would invite them for an interview, and it breaks my heart.

Advice on finding and applying for jobs is plentiful, but it tends to focus on *format* (the form for a cover letter, a template for a resume). What I provide here you might not find as readily—advice on the *attitude* you should bring to those difficult rhetorical tasks.

---

*And a date! And a raise! Just before publication, I used these strategies to write a letter to buy my first house. (Adulting!) The owners accepted our offer within hours—well below the asking price. The agent said their eagerness had much to do with how I wrote that letter.

I won't be dispensing information you can easily google (checklists, spreadsheets to keep track of your job search, time management strategies) or learn at your campus career center (how to discover if a workplace is toxic, whether to cover your tats or remove your nose ring for an interview, what to expect in a negotiation).* Instead, this book is about the *mindset* that leads to success in the job search. I want to help you think about your job search—who you are, what you value, and how to channel Goldilocks† to find a job that's "just right"—and then show you how to convey those things in your written materials and your interactions with potential employers.

To write the book, I called on dozens of smart people with different kinds of expertise in the hiring process: campus career office directors, tech start-up founders, lawyers, librarians, corporate communications experts, CEOs, CFOs, UFOs (kidding), physicists, physicians, publishers, hedge fund managers, journalists, bankers, small-business owners, chefs, engineers, copywriters, ranchers, marketers, military officers, and of course human resources professionals. You'll meet many, though not all, of them in these pages. Because they were candid in our conversations, you'll get unvarnished thoughts, sometimes in delightfully salty language. Often they used the same words to express identical ideas, so I edited to avoid too much repetition. But the main takeaways are there. Lots of it was a revelation to me and will probably surprise you too.

Before becoming a writing professor, I had been on the deciding (or "hiring") side of the desk for many years, first as an acqui-

---

* Career center professionals can also connect you with alumni, do practice interviews, and help you set up your LinkedIn profile (a necessity). These offices are full of resources and, strangely, not enough students take advantage of them.

† Except you do not want to emulate that spoiled, breaking-and-entering, privileged little brat who ate others' stuff, slept in their beds, and still complained. Fairy tales don't always provide good examples of how to behave.

sitions editor in scholarly publishing and later as an undergraduate admissions officer at Duke. Crafting personal statements for college applications is hard, and many students get bad advice. The same is true with job materials. But writing well is a teachable and learnable skill, and that's where I come in.* Evaluating applications when there are many qualified candidates can be deeply subjective. This is also true for hiring, and you'll see I use comparisons between college admissions and the job search throughout this book.

Dating may provide an even more apt analogy. While plenty of students end up perfectly happy attending their safety school, romantic relationships depend on chemistry. While the job search may feel one-sided to you—as if the employer has all the power—it's actually about finding a good match. It's in both parties' interest to be as honest and up-front as possible so there are no nasty surprises. Everyone wants a happily ever after.

There's an ugly truth here. While the world may slowly be changing, thanks in large part to those committed to fighting for social justice, it's no secret that women, people of color, and especially women of color, still have to work twice as hard to be deemed half as qualified for jobs they're well equipped to do. BIPOC (and queer folk and those with disabilities and poor people and immigrants and anyone from a group that has suffered discrimination) may have to deal with tokenism, impostor syndrome, exploitation, and aggressions—micro and humongous—those with privilege will likely never encounter.

We all need to do a bit of code-switching in different environments, but some face greater challenges than others. No book will be able to level what is more of a ski slope than a playing field. My

---

*My previous book was *Write Your Way In: Advice on Crafting an Unforgettable College Admissions Essay.* If you want to know more about writing well in the first person, you can check it out. Much of the advice there holds true for cover letters.

hope is that information here will be especially helpful to those who may not have access to family and friends with deep pockets and wide webs of connections.

When you're searching for a job, you must do enough research, interviews, and poking around to know if you'll be comfortable. "Fit" is a term you'll hear in hiring, though not much from me. I prefer "match." That's because sometimes "fit" is used to say "You're not one of us." If your Spidey sense tells you something's hinky, listen to it the way you would on a Tinder date. Get the hell out.

The reader I have in mind—the "you" I address—is a recent or soon-to-be college grad. But the advice I've gathered from experts holds true for many others. I hope this book will be useful to parents who want to help their children and to professors who understand that part of our work *should* include helping students get ready for careers. While my focus is on snagging first jobs, the fundamentals of communication also hold true for seasoned executives seeking new leadership positions.*

While interviewing, I kept hearing the same complaints. But when I shared with students and recent job seekers what I'd learned, they were shocked. No one had ever told them this stuff. They realized they were doing the exact things that would keep them from getting hired.

I want to help you think about what you need to be successful in the job search. The title of the book offers a formula to address potential employers. Tell them why you are interested in working for them (*why you*). Then tell them how, based on your attitude and experiences, you can help and support their mission (*why me*). You might initially get the order wrong and want to put

---

*When I served on a hiring committee for a new provost at my university—the chief academic officer—I was shocked by how bad, and I mean *bad*, some cover letters from well-respected scholars were.

yourself first. That's understandable. But if you think about it for a moment, you'll realize it's kind of rude to barge in with a self-interested approach. And putting *you* before *me* will set you apart as an applicant. And finally, emphasize how ready you are to try to contribute (*why now*).

It goes to the main thing I want to help you with: how to present yourself—as respectful, eager, and curious or, in the words I've heard tons of employers use, humble, hungry, and smart. I'll define the attributes employers say they're looking for and teach you how to present them on the page.

But first I'll show you a bunch of mistakes you may not even know you're making.

Introduction

You've found a website that lists lots of job postings or landed on the Careers section of a company you'd love to work for. All you have to do is upload your cover letter and resume and submit them. Easy, right?

Let's slow down and consider what happens after you click Submit.

When you apply online your material will be scanned, and the fancy formatting on your resume—the colors you've added to make it stand out, the little curlicues and cute graphics you've worked so hard on to represent who you are—will be converted to simple text so it looks identical to those of all the other applicants. The information you provided will be delivered at the speed of electrons to R2-D2.

Okay, so not exactly R2-D2. But when I first learned that more than 70 percent of resumes submitted online are immediately rejected by AI bots, I got a mental picture of everyone's favorite robot from *Star Wars*.

Here's what I imagine. That shiny little guy stands at a console and picks up your resume. If it's not in a format his ATS (applicant tracking system) programming can read, his head swivels around, he makes sad squeals, and then he incinerates your document.

If he can read it, he holds it in one appendage, shoots out another arm (or whatever), and compares it with the employer's list of job requirements. His bullet head goes back and forth between the job description and your resume. Each time he finds a word or phrase that matches *exactly*, a bulb goes on and he emits a whistle of delight. But if only four lights go on when the list contains fifteen items, he utters a gloomy *oooh*, and out comes the flamethrower.

When resumes have enough of the right matching words, the little bot lights up like a Christmas tree, swivels around in a happy dance, and transmits them to a human. *Hooray!*

The path to success in many endeavors, including being a good person, is to practice imaginative empathy—to work hard to understand what life is like for other people. That's one reason we read literature. This is also a way to get what you want. If you can picture someone else's struggles, you can ask for things in a way that makes it easy for them to say yes.

Imagine, then, a manager who needs to hire an assistant. We'll call her Olivia.*

What it's like on the other side of the hiring desk

Olivia is tired. So tired. Her voicemail is full, and the number of unread emails in her inbox is in five digits. She's up against a deadline, and because she's down a staff member, she has to do both her job and that person's job. Her boss is out of town, so she has to schedule and run meetings. Plus, her partner just had a baby so no one in the house is sleeping.

---

*I am picturing Olivia Pope, the political "fixer" played by Kerry Washington on the TV show *Scandal*. She hired a bunch of people who weren't exactly mainstream because she saw strengths and skills (killing, breaking and entering, illegal taping) that wouldn't show up on a resume. She called them her "gladiators." She also wore great clothes.

The staff member who'd been her assistant was super competent, so Olivia promoted them to another role. Olivia cares about the people she hires, and she goes out of her way to help folks advance in their careers, within her organization or elsewhere. She loves mentoring young people, and they appreciate how much they learn from her. Her most recent assistant helped write the job description so the new person would have the necessary skills to make Olivia's life easier. But without that person? Olivia is drowning in work.

And she's drowning in resumes. A listing on LinkedIn has netted more than two hundred resumes a week. Though the job ad said a cover letter was optional, Olivia prefers applicants who take the time to write one. Those letters help her understand the applicants' personalities and decide if she wants to meet them. So she skims the letters first. She's been doing this work for days now, and (Did I mention?) she's tired.

Olivia doesn't bother to read anything longer than one page. If she spots more than a few typos or spelling errors, into the trash the letter goes. Letters from applicants who say they are applying for a job at a different organization (oops) or don't mention the specific job she listed—into the trash.

Each time she sees "I am the most qualified applicant for this job," she snorts and puts the letter aside. *No, you're not,* she thinks. *You have no idea how strong the pool is.*

When she reads how this job would be a good stepping-stone toward an applicant's future plans, her colleague down the hall hears her exclaim, "No kidding! I know exactly why this job is good for you. Tell me why you're good for this position. I need someone to help me get through this big honking pile of work!"

Her eyes glaze when she sees the same meaningless words and phrases: passionate, committed, hardworking, detail-oriented, driven. *What on earth does that look like in the experiences you've*

*had? And why didn't you apply some of that passion to proofreading
your materials, or ask a truly detail-oriented person for help?*
These reactions may seem harsh. And to a degree they are.
But if your application materials represent your best effort when
you have loads of time to think about how you present yourself
and could have taken advantage of opportunities to get help, mistakes in grammar and punctuation and spelling should not happen. If you can't impress under these tame circumstances, how
will you perform under pressure, on deadline, and when the organization's reputation is on the line?

As with the cover letters, Olivia doesn't read resumes longer
than one page. If they don't include contact info, or if it's hard
to find? Into the trash. If she can't figure out how a candidate's
experience sets them up to do the job? Trash. She doesn't try to
decipher anything with fancy typefaces or lines of information
that crawl vertically up the page. The trash bin is getting full.

If someone attended seven colleges before finally graduating?
Well, Olivia understands life can get in the way of school. But if
they've offered no explanation? Trash. If a candidate describes
simple tasks with overblown language ("Escorted canines to relief
stations"), she laughs and shows the document to the colleague
down the hall, who will also find it hilarious. The resume goes
into the trash, but Olivia knows they'll mention "canine relief" to
each other for years to come, whenever they see anyone walking
a dog.

For those who take up valuable real estate on their resumes
with lists of references, she feels sad and thinks, *Why? We're not
at that stage yet!* She also wonders about too much blank space.
Surely a person did something—worked in a warehouse, operated a cash register, babysat a younger sibling. Those experiences
could tell her a lot, especially if the candidate makes clear what
they learned. Why wouldn't those be listed?

If hobbies include riding dressage or earning a private pilot's license or acquiring a PADI scuba certification, but the applicant lists no work experience or internships, Olivia figures the resume has come from a child of privilege who's gotten everything they ever wanted and probably doesn't need to work. She knows that's her personal prejudice and knows, too, that other managers may see those hobbies and think, *Hey, this person is just like me!* She's been in the business world long enough to know most people like applicants who remind them of themselves in some way. And she's lived long enough to know that life isn't fair.

Olivia's job list includes "must haves" and "nice to haves." She skims for the qualifications she knows she needs. If someone says they know Microsoft Excel or Adobe Illustrator, she wonders how proficient they are and why they haven't listed experience to back up those claims. She gives a little cheer for applicants who've earned industry-recognized certifications.

When she's winnowed the pile to a bunch of promising applicants, she gives up, turns off her computer, and leaves the office. She started out tired. Now she's exhausted and, to be honest, kind of pissed off. As she walks to her car, she feels annoyed that so many recent college grads wrote only about what they wanted from the job. Few of them had done real research into her organization or even addressed their letters to her personally. *How could you know you're the right match or the "ideal candidate" and want to work here if you seem to know nothing about this job or company or the skills we painstakingly listed in the job description?*

How did they get to be so self-centered? And cocky? Confidence is fine. It can be essential in many jobs, especially sales. But most of these applicants came off as downright arrogant. Who wants to work with someone who thinks they're all that? Not Olivia. *It's not about you,* she thinks before she drags herself to bed. *I don't care about you and what you want.*

Yet. True, Olivia doesn't give a hoot about applicants she will never meet. But she will come to care for the person she eventually hires. She always does. She works hard to find a good match, someone who shares the values of her organization and would be an asset. She knows they will come in without specific skills, and she'll have to make an investment in teaching them before they can truly contribute. She values employees who ask lots of questions; those people she would mentor and promote.

Maybe, she thought as she lay awake, stressed because she needed to hire someone as soon as possible, *these recent grads just don't know what they don't know when it comes to applying for jobs.* Maybe no one taught them how to approach the process, how to be professional.

The next day, eager to give applicants the benefit of the doubt, and with the understanding that writing resumes and cover letters is hard for everyone (and realizing the ones who made it to the top of her pile had probably been smart enough to seek help), Olivia was excited to start talking to candidates. Normally she would send an email inviting an applicant to set up a time to talk, but she was desperate to get someone in place and, in any case, the job sometimes required cold-calling clients, so she skipped that step.

The first person's phone rang and rang and finally went to voicemail. The outgoing message sounded as if it was recorded at a party. Olivia ended the call. She tried the next person and got no answer until an automated message informed her the voicemail was full. She finally got through to the fifth person on her list, who answered with "Yo!"

Once Olivia explained who she was and why she was calling, the applicant quickly changed tone. She asked, "So, why do you want to come work for us?" The answer: "Well, I need a job." Thanks, but no thanks.

The next candidate seemed more promising, and they had a good chat—until Olivia asked if they had any questions and they said, "Can you tell me about your company?" Olivia thought, *Seriously?* as she ended the call. The next person had a lot to say. So much, in fact, he interrupted and talked over her. Out.

She did get a panicked phone call asking if all the materials had been submitted and how they looked. That would have been fine if the caller had been the applicant. It wasn't. The applicant's mother was calling to check up on her son. Olivia wondered if Mom was planning to come to work with him too.

The series of ten-minute phone calls had given her a headache.

After a few days Olivia had found some people she thought highly enough of to invite for interviews with her and a few members of her team.

The first person never showed. *I've been ghosted*, Olivia thought. *No. Couldn't be.* When she called to see if he was okay, he said, "Oh, I got a better offer." She made a note in her files in case he ever applied for another job at her organization.

The next person came in and impressed Olivia and her colleagues with her professionalism and the way she spoke about her experience. Before the interview she had asked for a list of the people who would be questioning her, which Olivia was happy to provide. The poised young woman had clearly done research on each of them and asked smart and appropriate questions that led to a terrific conversation. But when Olivia asked the receptionist for her input, the longtime employee and valued team member said the applicant had failed to hold the door for someone coming in behind her with an armful of packages. Then she talked loudly on her phone while waiting for the interview. When the receptionist asked her to lower her voice, she was rude. Out.

Another person, even more qualified, gave a wowser of an interview. She spoke with excitement and dedication about what she wanted to do in her career and the mission that drove her. Unfortunately, none of what that candidate talked about had anything to do with the work at Olivia's organization.

The next applicant was so anxious he sweated through his shirt. Everyone on the interview team told him it was fine to be nervous, completely understandable, and he could stop and take a breath. When he finally calmed down and was asked about the work-study job he had in college, he talked about how demanding his boss was and how unfairly he'd been treated. He said he'd hated every minute of working for that supervisor. Out.

A candidate whose resume listed an impressive achievement, when asked to explain what he'd contributed to the results, was forced to admit he'd been just one of a dozen team members, and it soon became clear he hadn't actually understood the project. Out.

For another candidate, a quick reference check revealed they hadn't even worked in the position listed on the resume.

One kept mentioning "our beach house in Cabo" and "our ski condo in Aspen." By "our" they meant their parents'. *Privilege is fine*, Olivia thought. *Entitlement isn't.*

Eventually the team narrowed the field to two promising candidates. In the final round of interviews, one said, "Just for funsies, when could I expect to be promoted?" Out.

The other finalist, whom they hired, showed up on the first day of work and said, "You know, I accepted the job, but I don't think I'm being paid what I'm worth. I think I should be making a higher salary." When they showed up the next day, Olivia told them it wasn't going to work out.

And then the cute little robot had to start screening resumes all over again.

While Olivia is fictional, all these hypothetical applicants made actual mistakes hiring managers have complained about. And most of these recent or soon-to-be college grads looking for their first real jobs didn't even realize how they had screwed up. It's hard to blame them (except in cases where they were just being rude). Most of us think about ourselves first. We think about what we want and how nervous and tired we are. And about how we really need to get a job—any job—soon. As soon as possible.

So we take shortcuts and send the same letter and resume in response to as many job postings as we can find that we may or may not be qualified for at places we may or may not know much about and may or may not want to work at. The more desperate we feel, the more mistakes we make. And all this effort leads nowhere or, more accurately, leads to the unfortunate scenarios above and to a sense of failure and depression for the candidate.

That's too bad. Because the truth is, employers want to hire you. Thinking of them as mean old gatekeepers or preparing for an antagonistic relationship where you feel you're going to be judged and found lacking is a mistake. Hiring managers don't want the process to drag out. They don't love saying no.* You can and should feel empowered about the job search if you adopt the right mindset and learn things you've yet to be taught.

You've probably been told you need to sell yourself. Let's con-

---

*When I was stopped for speeding (yes, I am an older white woman and so got off easy) and went to Bad Driver's School, one of the cops said, "We're not sitting there hoping you're speeding so we can give you a ticket. We don't like giving tickets. We just want you to obey the law." That, among other things I learned on a summer afternoon, was a valuable insight. It's a good reminder of the mindset required to be successful at job hunting, even though the rules are not posted on big signs along the highway.

sider that for a moment. How do you like it when someone is trying to sell you something you may not want or need? Have you ever been stopped while hurrying to a class or an appointment by someone who wants you to sign a petition for an issue you don't care about? When hiring managers are looking to fill a job, they know exactly what they need. They've spent hours crafting a job description and deciding where to post it to attract the most qualified candidates. In other words, they've thought about it. How can you do the same for them?

Let's get this straight. I'm pretty sure you're amazing in ways you're not even aware of. My hunch is you have much to offer the world and once you find the right job you'll be a terrific employee. That's where I'm starting from. I want to help you understand some things you may not yet know you don't know.

Your family may have told you that you are special and unique. They may have said you can be anything you want to be. They may have made you feel like the center of the world—a celebrity—and claimed all you have to do is believe in yourself to find success in whatever you do. I hope you've had a supportive family; it makes life easier.

It's also possible all you ever heard were words of criticism. You've worked hard to prove your worth not only to the doubters but also to yourself. This can be even more of a challenge for many of us.

Your teachers may have told you you're smart and talented. Or perhaps you've been consistently underestimated and led to believe you were good at nothing. I know that's not true. Maybe you just haven't discovered what you love doing. When you find that, I'll bet you'll excel.

For college admissions essays, you were asked to write about who you are and what makes you special. What did you want to study? Which clubs and organizations would you join? Maybe you lucked out and got into your first-choice college. More likely, you ended up loving your safety school. Maybe you decided to save money and attend community college. Perhaps you've opted out of higher education altogether. The truth is, it doesn't matter as much as you might think when it comes to careers.*

In college, your professors looked over your work, praised what you did well, then showed you how you could perform even better. You may not have had personal relationships with all of them, but I hope you found some mentors willing to chat whenever you stopped by their offices as you transitioned away from family into a life that was more independent, more of your own making.

Even if your story varies in the particulars and you worked your way through school doing minimum-wage jobs and taking care of younger siblings or traveling every weekend to visit ailing grandparents, the bottom line is at this point you've been conditioned to feel like it should all be about you—your hopes and dreams, your wants and needs, your quest to develop into the person you (and others, like me) know you can be.

Here's some hard news: When you start applying for first jobs, no one cares about you. No potential employer wants to hear what you want or why the position they're trying to fill is good for you. It's not about you.

There's one question every potential employer asks themselves. *How will hiring you make my job easier?* It's that simple.

---

*Some type-A parents won't believe this, but employers—even in industries that used to be the snobbiest about which colleges their employees attended (*cough*: investment banking, consulting, white-shoe law firms)—care a whole lot less about those brand names these days. Majors matter mostly to university department chairs, and minors count for bupkis in the real world. In today's climate, many employers say they're happy to hire applicants without degrees if they can show they have useful skills.

Of course you will continue to develop and grow, and you need to keep firmly in mind your values, passions, and goals. But when it comes to *applying for jobs*—and I'll repeat this even though it might sound harsh—*no one cares about you and what you want to do.** They want to know what you can do for them.

The key to a successful job search is to adopt a mindset foreign to many college students and recent grads, an approach that shows employers you are focused more on contributing to their organization than you are on yourself.

In this book I will show you what that mindset looks like on the page in your cover letters and resumes and in the interview room. I will help you avoid mistakes you may not know you're making.

Someone somewhere told young people it was important to be full of confidence and to sell themselves.

Oy.

Nothing is less appealing than a person whose swagger far exceeds their abilities. When employers look to hire, it's easy to blow apart puffed-up claims of expertise and to expose, if not outright lies, at least exaggerations. And let's face it, unless you're the one seeing all the applications, there's no way you can assess how you might stack up against other candidates. I'll start by begging you, please, never claim you're well qualified—or, worse, *the most qualified*, or *the best fit*, or *the perfect person* for the job. Even if you are, which you may be, let the employer come to that conclusion.

---

*Well, I care about you! That's why I wrote this book. I care especially about people who don't have access to all the goodies, people who are the first in their family to attend college and don't have anyone to help them with all this stuff. If you're in that position and are reading this book in a library, bookstore, or career office and can't afford your own copy, write me a good email (racheltoor@gmail .com). You may need to keep reading to find out what a "good email" looks like, though.

You know what's a winning strategy? Sending this message: "I know I don't know enough yet, but I'm eager to work hard and learn as much as I can to be able to contribute to your mission." You don't have to know everything (or even, really, a lot). If you can present yourself as eager and curious and willing to bust your butt, you'll rise to the top of the applicant pool. Seriously.

People who hire for entry-level positions all say the same thing: Recent graduates have no idea how to present themselves professionally. The best applicants make silly mistakes. The worst—braggy, overconfident, and demanding—have employers wondering, *Who do these kids think they are?*

Well-loved children who were told they could be and do anything? Maybe. Or perhaps they've just never been shown how to write professional communications. I try not to blame people for things they haven't yet been taught. Like many professors, I always spend a few minutes on the first day of class talking to students about how to email a professor. My name is not "Hey," I tell them. Neither is it "Hi" or "Hello." If I get a message, I want to know it's directed to me. I prefer that students call me Rachel. But before I tell them that, they should default to something more formal and polite, like Professor Toor.* It helps when they use a subject line that lets me know what they need from me. And when they remind me which class they're taking.

In college there is a "hidden curriculum"—a set of unwritten, rarely discussed rules and practices—many professors don't even think about teaching to students. Somehow they expect you to figure it out on your own. My first week of college I had no idea I

---

*Some students are not comfortable calling professors by their first names, so for those who've been in my class for a while, I give them the option of addressing me the way my phone does—as "Your Highness." Surprisingly few have taken me up on this offer.

was supposed to go to the bookstore to buy required texts for my courses. I didn't know how to register for courses or realize I could withdraw. I thought professors' office hours were only for those who needed extra help, so I never took advantage of them.* I relied on friends to show me what was expected.

The hidden curriculum in applying for jobs has little to do with finding the right format and font for your resume and everything to do with mindset and attitude. I tell students, "Writing is easy. Thinking is hard."† In this book I focus on the thinking. If you can keep in mind the main question an employer will ask themselves (How will hiring you make my job easier?) and adopt a mindset of wanting to contribute, you are more likely to be successful. I will give you Practical Pro Tips and exercises to help you prepare. At the end of each chapter, since I know many people now belong to the tl;dr‡ club, I'll provide a series of Quick Takes. If you've read this far only because your parents bought the book since they're desperate for you to stop playing video games and get a job, at least look at those summaries, which might help you avoid the really stupid mistakes. For the insecure overachievers (*Love you, peeps!*), there's a little treat at the end where I dish out my tools and tricks for writing well (and concisely).

As I've already mentioned, the title of the book provides a simple formula for your cover letter. I'll explain what that looks like in practice. I'll tell you the most important task while preparing a resume is figuring out how to translate what you've already

---

*Office hours are there for you to have a chance to interact with your professors and get to know them. Every student should take advantage of these opportunities to exploit faculty members for all they're worth. Plus, we like getting to know you.
†Okay, the truth is both writing and thinking are hard.
‡Too long; didn't read.

done into what the job you're applying for requires. I'll cover ways to prepare for interviews and actions you might take to follow up (hint: thank-you notes aren't just for birthday presents from grandparents).

If you do everything right—and really, there are a lot of strategies to do this well and more ways to go wrong—know that it can take a lot of hard work to get work. This can be a long, exhausting, and demoralizing slog. Your first job will probably be just that— a first and not a last. You are likely to have many more. Learning to think about job applications now will help you throughout your entire career.

Everyone wants to know the recipe for the special secret sauce that will help them succeed. Here it is again: *How will hiring you make my job easier?*

But consider this. You are about to embark on an exciting journey. The job search provides a great opportunity to figure things out about yourself: What do you care about most? What are your core values? What kind of mission do you want to contribute to? In the process of looking and applying, doing research and informational interviews, you have a chance to meet a lot of interesting people. This will help you expand your world and introduce you to careers you'd never thought of. Sure, it'll be a lot of work, but if you treat it as an adventure and an opportunity for self-discovery, it could also be a boatload of fun.

Just as going to college presented one kind of transition, probably some combination of terrifying, fantastic, and—during the pandemic—just plain weird, entering the workforce is another major step most of us take on the road to independence. Greet that challenge with as much enthusiasm as you can muster. The goal is to end up at an organization where you will learn a ton, fill a need, and feel supported and appreciated.

Quick Takes

- Mindset matters more than skills.
- Keep in mind the question, How will hiring you make my job easier?
- Saying you don't yet know but are eager to learn is more effective than asserting you're a good fit.
- Figure out how to translate what you've already done into what the job you're applying for needs.
- Use the job search to explore things you're really interested in pursuing.

1 *Attitude*

I told you about a fictional hiring manager named Olivia because through reading we learn about the experiences of people different from us. Empathy is perhaps the most important quality you can develop.

Fred Rogers was a paragon of empathy. In his long-running TV show *Mr. Rogers' Neighborhood*, he showed us a grown-up remembering how it feels to be an overweight, introverted, sickly child. No matter how successful he became, Mr. Rogers never forgot what it was like to be overlooked, and he never stopped being humble. His deep empathy allowed him to make real and meaningful connections. Mr. Rogers showed us what it's like to be a righteous person, a mensch, and to realize everyone we meet can teach us something.

He also said, "What's mentionable can be more manageable." That's great advice in life, and it's especially apt for the job search. No one expects you to be perfect. You may have messed up. There may be things in your past you're ashamed of. You're human. What matters is how you present your goofs and flaws to the world. Giving examples of mistakes that show how you've learned and grown is a winning strategy.

Character—the mental and moral qualities and traits that define us—turns out to be one of the most important factors in getting hired. When you start out, you may not have all the skills and competencies listed in the job description. You may, in fact, have few of them. What you do have is your attitude and how you demonstrate your character.

Now, you just can't fake certain things. If you're shy and soft-spoken, you can work to overcome that and practice using your outside voice indoors, but you may never be comfortable speaking to a roomful of strangers. If you're naturally exuberant and noisy, a job that requires you to sit alone in a quiet room for hours will likely make you miserable. You are who you are. It's your task to know yourself and to find a work environment that allows you to feel comfortable. There are places for introverts and extroverts and everyone else—most of us—who falls somewhere in between.

As I interviewed employers, recruiters, and hiring managers in vastly different industries, they all kept saying the same thing. They said they looked for people who were humble, hungry, and smart, often using those exact words. Only after I had finished all the interviews did I discover the "HHS" process used by management consultant Patrick Lencioni in his best-selling 2016 book, *The Ideal Team Player*.* Like most brilliant ideas, Lencioni's stress on the character traits essential for being a good employee—humble, hungry, and smart—was so obvious, once he articulated it, the notion seeped into the air of the workplace and was passed on without mention of, or perhaps even knowledge of, the original source.

In what follows I'll give you my take on these qualities based on my interviews with people in a position to hire you.

---

*Do yourself a favor and watch Lencioni's TEDx Talk. You'll see that once you get a job, there are many ways you can go wrong if you don't bring the right mindset to work.

Humble: It's not about you— it's about how you can contribute

Humility doesn't come naturally to all of us, especially if we've been able to find success without having to work hard. You might be afraid that if you don't talk about how great you are, no one will realize your worth. But you risk coming off as braggy. Though I'm sure you're worthy of a position at a top company, realize you're not all that valuable to an employer. *Yet.*

A mindset shift will require thinking about the situation from someone else's point of view. You're no longer at home or in college, where for the most part things *are* about you and your growth. Out in the world, no one cares if you were a joint-rolling genius or wants to hear about your exploits in the rodeo ring— unless you can show how that will allow you to excel at the specific job you're applying for. Again, the message: It's not about you or what you want to do, or even what you've already done in different arenas. It's about showing how hiring you will make someone else's job easier.

Everything you've been told about how to confidently sell yourself? Forget it. What's appealing is a person who knows they don't know enough—*yet!*—but can balance that with confidently describing their experiences and skills as well as demonstrating their abilities and their interest in learning more.

It's easy to sniff out a faker. That attitude makes the jerk in me push to expose fraud. Generally I can tell in about four minutes if someone is full of doggie doo. And so can most employers. You don't want that to happen to you.

One of the best skills you can develop in life is the courage to say, "I didn't know that." Even better is to follow up with, "Can you tell me more?"

Hungry: Enthusiasm gets you far

Artists who do well need two important qualities: talent and discipline. The latter is the more difficult to come by. I can give you a short list of successful writers who wait for the muse to strike before they sit down to write. And I can give you a long list of people who put their butts in the chair and get to work. Every day. Even when they don't feel like it. *Especially* when they don't feel like it. Those are the authors whose works line the shelves of libraries and bookstores and the artists whose paintings hang in museums and galleries.

By *hungry* employers mean eager, enthusiastic, and willing to work hard. They want to hire folks who are ready to do whatever it takes and are willing to work to compensate for being a drain on resources until they become skilled enough to contribute. I've heard the same thing from engineers to ranch managers to media executives: when you're first hired, someone will have to take time away from their own work to train you. It may take weeks or months before you're of any value. During that time, the organization takes a productivity hit. That's why it's so important for employers to find new recruits who have the right mindset and are not arrogant jerks who think they already know it all.

In a first job, actually in any job, you have to get through the grunt work without complaint—even the most glamorous jobs have a big ratio of drudgery to fun—and then be ready for new challenges. Good bosses, instead of being threatened by a younger, faster, stronger version of their former selves, will value an employee whose secret desire is to replace them. If a supervisor works late in the office, you'd do well not to be the first to leave and hit the bars. Good bosses will tell you where you're falling short—with the goal of helping you improve, not making you feel bad (though that might be an unintended side effect, so you need to learn to take feedback well). Good bosses will see how much work you're doing and help you up the ladder. They will become your champions. They'll be sorry to see you move on but are likely to remain mentors and even become friends.

Enthusiasm comes in different flavors. For some, like me, it can involve talking quickly, a flapping of arms, and a long string of sentences that start with "And, and, and here's another thing!" But it's also okay to have a calm demeanor and really pay attention, to ask questions that show you are listening and making connections. In personal relationships we tend to look for people whose strengths complement our own. Hiring managers want employees who can fill various roles on a team by bringing their authentic personalities to work.

You might find my flapping and squawking uncool. (It *is* decidedly uncool.) But the opposite of enthusiastic is jaded and bored. A young person who acts like they already know everything is not appealing. Employers want to see you are eager to work hard and will embrace challenges with excitement.

Smart: Showing you're more than your scores and grades

How do you tell if someone is smart? The answer is unlikely to be found in perfect SAT scores and a great GPA and honor society memberships and Latin words after your degree. It also isn't knowing heaps of easily searchable facts and figures. Smart is about genuine curiosity, an ability to make educated guesses and forge connections: a desire to figure things out and to know more.

One good way to tell if someone is smart is to pay attention to the questions they ask. "How does that thing work?" "Who are you and how did you get to do the things you do?" "Why is this the process you follow?" "What's that place like?"

Scientists and engineers tend to be curious. A friend who owns a technical sales firm told me about a visit to a client whose company had invented a new way to get dents out of airplanes. I didn't quite get the details, but apparently it's not the way body shops fix cars. This company had developed a patented process. The owners brought him downstairs and showed him the machine.

My friend walked over to it and asked questions about how it worked. As soon as someone started to explain, he had more questions. He got excited.

His client told him this was part of their vetting for job applicants. "We bring them down here, show them the machine, and see how they react." If my friend had been looking for a job, it would have been his.

People tend to ask very few questions. Or at least few good ones. Every teacher will tell you the last thing they want to hear from a student is whether this material will be on the test. That is not a good question. A better question might be, "How does this connect to what we just finished studying?" Or "Can you give me a real-world situation where I might be able to use this knowledge?" (Only if not asked sarcastically.) Smart means curious.

Another friend hires scientists and engineers. If they make it through the initial screening, he takes them to lunch. After the candidate has ordered food (Have they thanked the server? Waited for everyone else to get their meals before digging in? Ordered the most expensive item on the menu? Asked for a cocktail or beer?), he watches to see if they salt the food before they take the first bite. He calls it the Thomas Edison test. I googled and found it's also ascribed to Henry Ford and other tycoons of industry.*

As my friend explained, the salt-before-tasting test reveals someone who makes assumptions, who thinks she already knows

---

*I fact-check. So do employers. In an age of "fake news," everyone should be in the habit of verifying sources and learning how to determine credibility.

something, who doesn't make decisions based on evidence or data. It displays a kind of arrogance: *I know what I like despite unfamiliar conditions.*

That example speaks to a fixed mindset not open to data. Many employers have told me what they really value is EQ: emotional intelligence. We all need the ability to read the room. Pouring salt on an unfamiliar dish sets up a dynamic. Are you careful and attentive to a situation? Do you pay attention to others? Can you work on a team? Does it show disrespect to the person in charge (the chef), who presumably knows how much seasoning a dish needs?

Curiosity may have killed thousands of felines, but it's what will help you get a job—and be successful. Organizations often develop ways of doing things. The executive assistant to the CEO of a big company, someone who's hired many staff members, told me the story of Grandma's ham, a kind of workforce parable: A young couple were having a ham for dinner, and one of them cut off both ends before cooking it. When his partner asked why, he said, "That's the way Grandma always did it." His partner, conscious of waste, asked again for reasons. He didn't know.

Although his grandmother had died, he called his grandfather and asked why his wife had cut off the ends of the ham. "Oh," he said, "because we had just one pan and that's the only way it would fit."

In other words, while originally Grandma had a reason to throw away perfectly edible meat, the young cook was carrying on a practice that was no longer necessary.

Many organizations do things equivalent to cutting off the ends of Grandma's ham. Most of us get into routines and eventually forget to ask the question favored by three-year-olds and physicists: *Why?* Why is that the way it's done? Is it policy or just habit?

Being smart does not mean you know more. No one wants to

hire a recent grad set on pointing out what the organization is doing "wrong." As you earn trust and responsibility, people appreciate questions that show a new perspective—like asking about Grandma's ham. Your suggestions (made with humility) may be valuable if you first honestly seek to understand the reasons behind things. That is, of course, the best way to remember the steps of a process—to make sure you know what needs to be accomplished and why each step is important.

Smart means being able to work smart. When you're given a list of tasks, you must triage—decide which is most important. You need to know where to go for help. You need, in fact, to be able to ask for help. That's not easy if you're focused on trying to prove your worth, but it makes you a much more valuable employee. No one will judge you for reaching out for more instruction.

Smart means being able to adjust to the culture of a place. If everyone else is draped in the apparel of the local sports team and has player bobbleheads on their desks, you probably don't want to wear the rival team's hat to work unless you can do it with a sense of humor and play.* It will be on you to figure out if the workplace culture is a match. That's essential, and I'll discuss it more in later chapters.

Ask smart questions. Smart means you don't preface statements with, "This may be a stupid question." If it's actually a stupid question, please, for the love of all that's holy, don't ask it. In my experience it's usually intelligent, competent women who undercut themselves this way. Not only are their questions rarely stupid, they're often about things everyone else also wants to know.

---

*I'm using sports here because it's easy, but imagine political examples that could really go wrong.

Instead of drawing attention to your insecurities and what you feel might be your intellectual weakness, why not just say, "Here's something I'm struggling with. Can you help me understand?" While no one wants to work with someone so full of themselves they proclaim they're the perfect candidate for a job, it's also hard to be around colleagues with so little self-esteem they apologize all the time. That just gets annoying.

The struggle to understand is beautiful. We all like to see people wrestle with ideas and problems until the light goes on. The honesty it takes to say you don't understand something gets us on your side and makes us want to help. This is what a growth mindset looks like: How hard are you willing to work to learn things that don't come easily to you?

What gets in the way of being able to say "I don't know" is shame. Often we have lingering humiliation from getting back tests and papers bloodied with red ink. If you volunteer an answer in class and the teacher says it's incorrect, you can feel like it's you who's wrong, not your answer. Please try to get over that.

Most scientists don't stake their identity on finding expected answers. They test and try and fail and start over. Most of the scientists—and writers and artists—I know spend a lot of time stuck. That's different from believing you're stupid, though sometimes feeling dumb comes with the territory. The key is being patient with a process that requires trial and error—and learning from errors. If you knew all the answers, what would be the point of attending college? The same is true with work. If you already have all the skills a job requires, you'll be bored out of your never-resting mind and want to quit on your third day.

Think about the mindset you bring to your job search. You will make mistakes, you will get stuck, and you will at times feel dumb. That's how most of us feel much of the time.

In school you may have figured out how to be successful. You could decide exactly how much (or little) effort you had to put in to get the grade you wanted. Professors gave you a rubric that told you what was required for each assignment. At the end of the academic term you knew where you stood and what you had left to do.

The job search is not so clear-cut. It's often a long slog with lots of dead ends and plenty of rejections. It's easy to feel overwhelmed and discouraged. It's normal, even. People say looking for a job is the hardest job you'll ever have. It may take longer than you'd like, and the first (or second or third) place you get hired might not be exactly the right choice for the long run. Along the way you'll understand how to be a good employee. And if it's not the right place, you'll look for another job using what you've learned on that first job and from this book.

Quick Takes

- The thing that matters most, and is totally in your control, is the mindset you bring to the job search.

- A mindset of "humble, hungry, and smart" not only will help you get hired, it will lead you to become a great team player for an organization.

2 *The Search*

If you have no idea what you want to do when you graduate from college, welcome to the club. It's a big one. The truth is many adults struggle to figure out how they want to spend their lives.* A lot of lawyers wish they could become finish carpenters. I had a boss in publishing who fantasized about working as a UPS driver. Many doctors would like to make art or study oceanography or write novels.

Most people do not start their dream jobs two weeks after graduation. Yet this is how everyone talks to college seniors. You'll be asked, "What are you going to do?" by family, friends, and even complete strangers. The question might make you feel as if you're already supposed to have it all figured out, know the answer, and show you're on the right path.

That's a load of hooey. Few get their dream job (whatever that is) right after college. And even if you did, how would you know about roads not taken, other possibilities better suited to your interests? The career journey for many people zigs and zags, which can be more interesting than a linear route. You may end up having ten, or twenty, or even more jobs during your lifetime, and new professional categories are popping up like morels after a

---

* Another truth is no one, no matter how old they are, ever really feels like an adult.

fire. Research shows that the first few jobs tend to direct a career path, but plenty of us have made big midlife changes.

It's best to let the job hunt start with thinking about what you've already done and whether you want to do more of it. This is one reason participating in student organizations, getting internships, or working summer jobs can lead to success after graduation. Having experience to fall back on can help you understand the kinds of things you might not like to do, but if you've never gotten to try something—or if, as is always the case, there are professions you haven't yet heard of—it's hard to narrow the field. If it feels like the whole world is open to you, choices can be overwhelming, like going into an ice cream store with too many unfamiliar flavors. Are you going to like cardamom better than sweet corn, or would you prefer dragon fruit sorbet?

The good news is your first job is not likely to be your last, and many of us switch careers and industries several times. But you have to start somewhere.

In college you may have taken random classes in subjects you knew little about. One mission of higher education is to teach people to think broadly about the world. Students are often encouraged to take a wide array of courses to see how different disciplines vary in their approach. At some point, however, you had to narrow your focus and choose a major. You may even have opted for more than one major. Maybe you threw in a minor or two.

If you regret your choices and think you should have studied business instead of philosophy or nursing instead of classics, don't worry. Most employers say majors and minors matter far less than attitude when it comes to hiring. You didn't make a bad decision. You learned how to think, you learned how to learn, and you learned how to meet deadlines.* It's rare that a job requires only one set of skills. For example, much of what you do as an en-

---

*If you didn't learn to meet deadlines, please start now.

gineering student (solve problems) applies to what you'll do as the manager of an advertising agency (solve problems). Philosophy majors learn to read critically and interpret arguments. That helps in pretty much any job, from park ranger to recording industry analyst to investment banker.

Campus career offices are gold mines

In the best case, you have diverse interests. It may be hard to figure out which to pursue to earn a living. People and tools are available to help you.

Start with your campus career center. The professionals who staff that office have valuable tools—personality assessments, interest inventories, apps that map majors to jobs—and have paid institutional subscriptions for them. While I don't list specific sites and apps in this book since they're likely to change, you can go to the career center and access them for free. And you can get advice from an actual person whose job is to help you find a job.

One of the most astonishing things I've learned in the course of my research is how few students take advantage of opportunities available to them. Only a small percentage visit their campus career offices. It might be because they don't know about them (some schools are better than others about supporting these centers and spreading the word). Or it might be because, as Ray Angle, Gonzaga University's assistant vice president for career and professional development, says, "They are scary places for a lot of students." Most students don't want to think about what they'll do after they leave the comfy collegiate nest. That's why so many use them as a "just in time" service. Ideally, charting a career path would start when you first arrive on campus and can gather information about all the resources, opportunities, and possible mentors available to you.

Campus career offices offer an abundance of help. They'll

work with you on cover letters and resumes. They may take a professional headshot for you to upload after they show you how to use LinkedIn and help you craft your profile; they can conduct mock interviews and give you feedback; they'll show you how to download job-search apps. Some have "closets" of clothes you can wear to interviews. They can also connect you to a vast network of alumni from your school already primed to talk to you.

You'll find out about deadlines for applying to various jobs and internships, and you'll learn which employers are coming to campus for recruiting events and when. You can attend general information sessions or have individual counseling and interview practice. Doing all this before the spring of your senior year will put you ahead of the pack.

Take advantage of every available opportunity. Even after you've graduated, you may still have access to your campus's career services for free.* When you've finished reading this book, or if you need a break, make an appointment at the career center. Then recommend that to your friends who are job hunting.

If you've heard that others have had a bad experience or didn't find the information they needed, realize that these offices, often staffed by excellent professionals, tend to be overlooked and underfunded when it comes to university priorities. Or it may be that things just aren't working for some people.

Michael Watson, a longtime human resources professional who has worked for Fortune 500 companies, big nonprofits, and government agencies, advises that if you are frustrated, try to make things better. He points out that college is the best place for

---

*No kidding. When I decided to apply to medical school, fifteen years after I got my BA, I called Yale to ask how to get my transcript. I discovered the pre-med adviser was available to help me with my applications. I applied, got in, and realized I didn't want to be a doctor. I remain grateful to Ed, the pre-med adviser, who was so gracious to a clueless alum.

students to learn to advocate for themselves. "Once they graduate and begin working," he cautions, "they will find that employers will not provide the infrastructure of support that colleges provide." Employees either perform or they risk losing their jobs or being placed on a slower track for future advancement. "In short," he says, "students have to be resourceful. Staying quiet when they are not getting what they need from Career Services will hurt them in their pursuit for internships and full-time jobs."

Network, network, network

Most people get jobs by networking. Around 70 percent of professionals get hired at places where they have some kind of connection. That means talking to a wide range of folks who may or may not be able to hire you. If you're lucky, you have family members with friends who work in a wide array of industries. But even if you don't, plenty of people a quick (thoughtful) message away will be willing to help an eager college grad. You'd be shocked at how much free advice is available to those who ask for it. I was. I've been awed by the generosity that even the busiest and most successful people are willing to show to strangers who reach out to them.

If you're like me, the idea of "networking" might seem kind of, well, slimy. But here's what I find appealing: it's an opportunity to snoop. As a writer, I often say I'm professionally nosy. It's in my job description to find people fascinating, and I do (they're my species!). I tend to ask anyone I meet a lot of questions, often in ways that are rare in those who are more reserved. If you were a Marine in Iraq or delivered pizzas or competed in barrel racing, I'll probably ask you about that. Most people are happy to talk about themselves if you express a genuine interest, and they often welcome a chance to reflect on how they got from there to here.

America's funniest founder, Ben Franklin,* learned the best way to get someone on your side is to ask for a favor. He won over a rival by writing a note saying that he knew the guy owned a rare book and asking if he could borrow it. The dude sent the book immediately, and Franklin returned it in a week with another note thanking him for the favor. The next time they met, Franklin says, "He spoke to me (which he had never done before), and with great civility; and he ever after manifested a readiness to serve me on all occasions, so that we became great friends, and our friendship continued to his death."

It's counterintuitive, the "Franklin effect," unless you remember that it's generally easier to give than it is to receive. If you ask someone for help—especially something easy for them to give—they will often go out of their way to be your advocate. The surprising part is that this is more effective than doing a favor for them. Don't be afraid to reach out to people you've never met and ask if they have five minutes to talk with you about their career path and offer some advice.

As I said, most people get jobs through other people. There's a cliché that it's not what you know, it's who you know. Like most clichés, it's true. The good news is in our online world, it's easier to find and get in touch with well-connected people than ever before. You no longer have to have attended the same schools, or country clubs, or polo matches.

If you want to understand how this works, google a classic *New Yorker* article by Malcolm Gladwell titled "Six Degrees of Lois Weisberg." Gladwell describes people he calls "connectors." He riffs on the game Six Degrees of Kevin Bacon, where you can trace how actors are connected to other actors and see most of them can be linked to Kevin Bacon. It has to do not just with how

---

*Franklin's autobiography, especially the first two sections, is a super fun read. Lin-Manuel Miranda left him out of *Hamilton* because he was afraid that, given his big personality, he'd take over the show.

many films Bacon's been in, but with the variety. That's the thing with connectors. They go wide in their contacts, not just deep. You won't necessarily know who they are, but if you learn to recognize them, they're invaluable. There are connectors among your friend group. You know, the ones who major in Chinese, do musical theater, play pickleball, and host parties where you meet people you want to get to know. The people who seem to know everyone.

How do you make connections and approach adults in a position to help you find a job? Start with people you already know and who will be low stress to approach. Do you belong to church or community groups? Do you have neighbors? Have you belonged to affinity groups in college? Clubs? Sororities or fraternities? Starting to network with folks closer in, then spreading out may feel less daunting.

You know your family. Do your parents have friends? Do they have siblings and extended family? There's some aunt on the other side of the country you may have met only a few times at weddings. Didn't she work at Lucasfilm or Disney? What about your father's nerdy college roommate, the one he says was always in the library? That guy went to medical school, then worked for a drug company that sold for a bazillion dollars. What's he doing now? Your dad says he's on the board of six start-ups. You want to get into med tech? Talk to that dude. Your grandma's high school friend, the girl voted most likely to succeed and did just that, working her way to the top of a giant corporation? She's now retired and is a workplace yenta who loves to make matches. Get in touch with her.

If your family doesn't have friends with upscale white-collar jobs or who do the kind of work you think you might be interested in, where do you turn?

Well, you know professors. Even if you were quiet in class, never took advantage of office hours, and don't feel you got to know any of your instructors well, if you reach out to them you may be surprised at how happy they'll be to help. Most of your professors know people who aren't professors. Let's see, off the top of my head I know lawyers, nonprofit directors, government employees, professional athletes, life coaches, graphic designers, CEOs, entrepreneurs, community activists, massage therapists, hedge fund managers, booksellers, editors, ambassadors, real estate tycoons, philanthropists, consultants, tech geniuses, college presidents, bakers, brewers, and breeders of organic beef. Your high school teachers have friends and family members who do things other than teach high school. Every person you know is connected to a network. Most people, if they stop to think for a nanosecond, should be able to put you in touch with someone if you ask nicely. (More on how to do that later.)

Talk to everyone you know about their jobs. It doesn't have to be a job you want to do and may even be something you've never heard of. You're collecting information. And it's never too early to start.

Wenda Cenexant, now a recruiter for a health care company, told me, "If I could go back in time I would network, network, network. I'd ask for informational interviews. I started doing that much later. My last semester in school I was taking six classes, volunteering, and working two jobs part time. I was pooped. I was basically on autopilot. It would have been hard to do that."

That may seem like a familiar scenario. You just don't have the time. And it's true, networking takes time—and also a boatload of emotional energy. But it's not that hard.

You have to reach out, but really, after an initial contact, mostly all you have to do is listen* and ask thoughtful questions

---

*And take notes. Make it a practice to take notes when you talk to anyone. Create a spreadsheet. Treat this job search like a gigantic research project, which is essentially what it is.

whose answers you can't find on Google. Start with those who are inclined to help you—family and friends and family friends and friends' family. Ask everyone you encounter for other contacts who might be willing to talk to you. Approach people with a range of jobs or a few fields—technology, education, manufacturing, import/export—you may be interested in and see what you can learn. Especially if you have no idea what you may want to do.

Contacting strangers

The best place to start may be your school's alumni network. It's easy to find happy alums who have already indicated they're willing to be contacted by recent grads. Your school serves as your introducer. You can write to someone and say you're a recent grad (or, even better, a current student) and you would love to hear about their journey after they left the mother ship. You can say you think you might be interested in working in advertising/ dog styling/pharmaceuticals and hope to hear about their experiences. Or you can just admit you'd like to make a connection.

These folks may want to reminisce about the good old days when they had snowball fights on the Old Campus or about how uncomfortable the beds were in Bingham Hall. Be prepared to respond patiently to remarks about how things have changed (now not only are the classes "co-ed" but the bathrooms are gender neutral), and make sure you keep the conversation focused on them.

It's good to approach people who share your interests. Maybe they too wrote for the school paper or played the same sports or also performed in step shows. Everyone likes to talk to people who are in some ways like them, though smart people tend to be especially interested in chatting with those who are unlike them. That's how we all expand our worlds.

Prepare a few questions in advance. How did you select this

field of work? What do you like about what you do? What steps should I take if I'm interested in pursuing a job in this field? It may also help to provide the contact with a copy of your resume to give them additional background information.

Think of yourself as a journalist doing a profile. Always prepare (Google is your friend). Take notes. Not just because you'll forget things, but because this shows you're serious and value their insights. At the end of the conversation, ask if you can contact them again if you have more questions. Keep them updated on your job search. Attorney and legal recruiter Robin Schachter says, "I love to hear from people I've spoken with in the past, especially when they have landed a job." This is how you build a network; everyone is flattered to be asked for advice, and many people like to think of themselves as mentors and helpers. Most of us received help along the way, and we like to pay it forward.

As I've said, people love to talk about themselves. They love to be asked questions that are easy to answer and to feel someone wants to listen. The problem is, we've become a nation of spouters. Often the students in my classes who know the least do the most talking. The really good ones stay quiet because they know that when you're talking, you're not learning.

Keep that in mind as you make connections. Your role is to listen, not to take up all their time talking about yourself. Some people will ask what you want. You should prepare a short answer along the lines of, "Well, I'm starting a job search and I'm trying to learn as much as I can about different professions [or, your field]." If the person you've approached holds a job you hope to have in the future, say, "I'm really intrigued by your work as a foreign service field officer, and I think it's something I'd like to do someday. Can you tell me what you did to get there?"

If they want to hear more about you, great. Offer some relevant bits you've thought about in advance. That helps you find common interests and connect in a meaningful way. But don't ramble on and on about the fantasy novel you want to write or how parking on campus stinks and you work a ton of hours and there's never enough time in the day to do all the things you need to do. In short, don't spend someone's precious time yammering about yourself.

This goes against our normal, natural, narcissistic inclinations. You have family and friends and peers who love you and will want to hear how overwhelmed you feel with schoolwork and whether your latest crush texted back. In the professional world, your gaze needs to be directed outward.

Collecting contacts

So you've asked each person you can think of for contacts. You can ask for names of people in particular fields or industries— say, publishing, or aerospace tech, or nonprofits—but early in the process it might be best to keep the search as broad as possible. If you're lucky and ask nicely, some especially helpful folks will say they're happy to provide an introduction. They'll send an email to you and to the contact giving each of you a little information. Here's something I might write:

> Jane, I'm writing to introduce you to Nadia, a recent college graduate who's interested in becoming a dog stylist.
>
> Nadia, this is Jane, who's had a long and impressive career styling dogs for such magazines as *Woof Woof Woof* and *Snarl*.
>
> I'm sure you two will have much to talk about, and I'll let you guys take it from here.

At that point you should thank me (the introducer), take me off the email chain, and ask Jane if she'd be willing to have a brief chat with you. But before you contact her, google her and google the two magazines I mentioned and discover as much as you can. I gave you that information because it will help you prepare for a better conversation. You can still ask Jane how she got interested in dog styling, what skills she developed before she got her first job, what she likes most about what she does, other career paths she considered following, and recommendations she might have for someone who wants to enter that field. At the end, you might ask if she can suggest others you might talk to. Keep a list of contacts, and like goldfish or sourdough starter, feed it so it grows.

In that way Jane might put you in touch with a friend who works as a zookeeper. Or a photographer who shoots vegetables for a glossy cooking magazine. Or someone who has a successful podcast talking to experts about training cats to be useful.* The point is, you don't know where this might lead. If you're open and you ask good questions, you're likely to learn something interesting.

What if your family are farmers and mostly know other farmers, and all you're sure of is you don't want to be a farmer? (Feel free to insert doctor/lawyer/restaurant owner or whatever.) What if what you want to do is something no one within your circle does—even though, as I've described it, this circle is possibly much bigger than you realize?

Then it's time to go beyond friends and family.

Google goes both ways

I get a lot of emails from strangers. Before I respond, I always google them. In the online world we're all friends, we're all

---

*It might be a fantasy of mine that cats could be as useful as dogs. Call me an optimist.

Practical Pro Tip: Social Media Check

Ask someone older than you—a relative, professor, parent of a friend—to do a social media check. Ask that person to google you and see if they find anything they think might be embarrassing. Tell them why you're asking, and listen to what they say without getting defensive or offering explanations or excuses. Remember, they're doing you a favor.

connected, we're all linked. Anyone you contact—including your future employer—may also have occasion to google you.

This is especially true if you're applying for a job that requires evidence of your skills, like graphic designer or dog stylist or journalist. They may expect to see samples of your taste in logos, your eye for fetching canine outfits, your articles. So go ahead and fill your social media feed with your work.

But most of us use social media for, well, more social things: That photo of your twenty-first birthday party where you and all your friends did a naked polar bear plunge chugging bottles of vodka? The posts about a sitting president, your underwear collection, your advocacy for the rights of squid? You should feel free to express yourself, show yourself, embarrass yourself as much as you want. But if you want to get a job, make those accounts private.

Some employers say they "try" not to look at a candidate's social media. But once you get past the bots, most employers are also human.

Sabrina Mauritz, who hires community activists, says, "Sometimes I use social media to confirm that I should *not* interview somebody. If they have a lot of skills but their ambition is about themselves, not about the field, I can get a confirmation for myself based on how and what they're posting on social media."

We are, for the most part, what we post. Philosopher José Ortega y Gasset wrote, "Show me what you pay attention to and I'll tell you who you are." Does your social media say the things about you that you want an employer to know? Are you sure?

Sabrina explains, "Have you worked for political opponents? I am going to want to know about that. I will check to look for people in common." Even in big cities, progressive politics is a small town. In good ways and bad: "If you're a dick and are blasting people and it's not centered in accountability," that's not good. "I don't care if people are drinking and stuff," she says, "but how messy are you? Are you airing all your dirty laundry? I don't want that drama, and I don't want the chaos."

Ellen Foltz, a recently retired high-level executive who has hired many people for the Fortune 500 companies she spent forty years working for, says social media is a big deal. People look at it before the first interview. Rarely, she says, will they do a dark web search, but Facebook, X, and LinkedIn are all fair game. People will get screened out for things like racism, sexism, and homophobia. Or, she says, "if they've posted all kinds of negative crap about their current employer. Not because you don't like your current employer but because you're an idiot." Your posts reflect your judgment as a human being. No one wants to hire someone who makes questionable choices—and then posts them publicly.

Go ahead and have a lively social media presence. But make private things private. Before you post something hateful about a public person, wonder how someone in a position to hire you would feel about it. How might the public person you're attacking feel? In the online world, people often forget the targets of their wrath are, in fact, people. Better not to be a troll, a hater. If you must vent, do it only to those who know and love you.

LinkedIn

LinkedIn is like Facebook* for work but without the divisive political rants, with fewer cute animal photos and less of the "if you lived my life you'd be happy" gloss. If you want to land a job, you kind of have to be on LinkedIn.

The site is a trove of useful resources. Search for people who do jobs you're interested in. Poke around. See what they post. Plenty of free content is available on the site about all kinds of career-related topics. You can sign up for a month's premium trial, take a bunch of online classes, and get industry-recognized certifications. Ultimately it might be worthwhile to invest in a membership.

Snoop around and find someone who seems, well, interesting. Someone you'd like to talk to.

Now here's where you have to think hard about your approach. I've told you people love to talk about themselves, and generally they'll be more than happy to speak to a young person. Remember what Ben Franklin taught you (via me, earlier in this chapter) about the best way to get someone on your side: ask a favor.

In this case, all you're really doing is asking for a conversation in which they talk about themselves. Should be no problem, right?

Well, it depends on how you ask. If you want someone to say yes, make it easy for them.

On LinkedIn, people are accustomed to getting requests from strangers. Glenn Gutmacher, director of talent sourcing at Huron Consulting Group, says you can go ahead and make a request. But

---

*Although you probably don't use Facebook, I bet your parents do. I assume you're at least familiar with it. And as with all social media, people's lives on LinkedIn are carefully curated.

if you just click "connect" with no text in the body, it looks random and will get rejected. Instead, he advises you add a note. It can be super simple:

> I'm a recent graduate of _____ and am very interested in [industry name]. Your organization has made great inroads in _____. [Relate your studies or interest up to that point]. I'd love to connect with you.

Make it noncommittal, Gutmacher says. You're not asking for a job. Not asking to meet for coffee. You just want to connect on LinkedIn. You can add, "At some point I would love to hear about your experiences in the field." It's a low-key ask without a big demand on the recipient.

Once they accept, you can see their contact information when you view their profile. That *is* a big deal. Now you have a way to reach them.

Wait a couple of days. Everyone likes enthusiasm, but no one wants to feel they're being stalked. Then you can send a message saying you'd love to continue the conversation. Ask for five minutes of their time. Gutmacher says, "Keep the burden of accepting as low as possible."

You've invoked a little bit of flattery by finding them, showing you know what they do and that you're not asking for much. Networking is about building relationships. LinkedIn was made for this kind of exchange. And remember, you've also accumulated a list of friends of family and family members of friends who might be able to help. Those people you'll have to contact through email.*

And yet. This can all go wrong. It can go wrong if you ask a

---

*Most older people still use email, and you'd be foolish not to check yours. I know many college students who have missed important deadlines and bursar's bills because they forget to check their email.

LinkedIn contact for a job in the first message. And it can go wrong if you don't approach someone in a way that gets them on your side. In fact, it was an incident with an email gone wrong that made me realize I needed to write this book.

Never be rude unintentionally: How not to approach a stranger

My college roommate is one of those connector people. This is a woman who stayed in touch with her second-grade teacher for forty years. She still sends holiday cards to a couple she met on a plane two decades ago. She knows people in pretty much every occupation you can think of, from baristas to chocolate company owners to award-winning documentarians to, well, I can't even imagine an industry where she doesn't know someone. She's the perfect person to ask for help.

Here's an out-of-the-blue message she got a few years ago, edited for anonymity.

[My friend's first name]:

I hope this email finds you well on such a dreary snowy day! My name's [her name is on her email] and I'm a recent graduate of [your college]. I was chatting with a friend of mine the other day about good newsletters and she suggested [your workplace]. After a skim of the website, I couldn't help but notice a fellow [alum] working in a leadership role there.

I wanted to reach out because I'd love to grab coffee and hear more about what you do. According to your LinkedIn, you've worn quite a few hats throughout your time there. I'm obviously pretty young but I feel like I'm already getting the urge to bounce around and learn more about different careers. Looking forward to picking your brain!

Practical Pro Tip: Making the LinkedIn Bots Work for You

At the beginning of your career, the free functions of LinkedIn will provide what you need. Nearly everyone in the hiring world uses this platform, so you need think hard about how you present yourself. Here's a breakdown of its various parts.

PROFILE

Your name: Use exactly the same name on resumes, applications, and LinkedIn. If you have a common name, use a middle name or initial or a nickname to distinguish yourself from others who appear in a search.

Title: Be creative, descriptive, or conversational in the title under your name. You don't need a formal job title; you can write, "Recent chemistry BS seeking lab or research role in pharmaceuticals" or "Marketing major eager to help your team use social media for growth."

Headshot: You don't need a formal photo, but what you post should not be blurry, should have a clean background, and should look like the person who will show up for a Zoom chat or job interview. It's legitimate to worry that you will be screened out (or in) based on your looks. This is yet another sad truth of the lousy real world. But profiles with photos appear higher in searches than those without because they're seen as more complete. Without a photo, some hiring managers may wonder what you're trying to hide. And since many companies look to expand the diversity of their workplace, they may seek folks from your cohort. If this makes you twitchy, you could replace a standard headshot with something like an avatar that syncs with your personality.

The banner behind the headshot: Don't overlook this valuable digital real estate, where you can distinguish yourself as someone thoughtful about their professional identity. You can use a photo, clipart, or diagram to convey something about you and your interests. If you can't think of anything specific, you can add a banner that's colorful and eye-catching.

Contact information: Use a professional-sounding email address (not drunkensot@aol.com) that's not tied to an institution (your college) or a current job. Set your LinkedIn account to receive messages. Allow notifications to go to an email address you check frequently. You can even create a dedicated account just for job searching and professional networking.

About: You should change this often, and you can use bullet points to highlight a few key skills and accomplishments. You don't need to write your whole life story or list every accomplishment—one paragraph will do. Just make it good. Try to use words and phrases from the kinds of job listings you're interested in to make it easy for bots or recruiters to scan.

Experience: In reverse chronology, list paid work, internships, and volunteer positions by the name of the organization, position/title, and dates. Add bullet points or a sentence or two to explain what you did. You can include membership on teams and in clubs and social groups, especially if you held leadership positions.

Education: List your most recently attended school and degrees earned first, and include honors, awards, and key extracurricular activities. Unless you have a top GPA (above 3.8, or above 3.5 in highly competitive schools or programs), you may want to leave it off your LinkedIn profile and resume.

NETWORK

You can ask to connect with anyone: friends, teammates, professors, work colleagues, supervisors, parents, family friends, relatives, and friends' parents. You need to get a critical mass of connections to make the LinkedIn algorithms work in your favor.

As you come across job postings, or companies you'd like to work for, enter the organization's name in the search bar, which should reveal the name and profile of any people you already know as first- or second-level contacts at that organization. Send a message to those people before you apply for the job. Remem-

(continued on following page)

**Practical Pro Tip: Making the LinkedIn Bots Work for You
(continued)**

ber, some may be able to receive a referral bonus. If you can connect with a current employee, you may be able to learn plenty of
relevant information. And you might also you hear about positions
not yet posted.

HAVE YOUR GENERIC RESUME READY TO GO

If you reach out to someone with a specific job posting in mind,
your LinkedIn contacts may ask for a resume. Before you send
anything, take a few minutes to modify it after your conversation.
If they ask for your resume before you talk you can say, "I'd like to
tailor it for your organization, so I'll be happy to send it to you after
we chat."

JOB POSTINGS

After you've completed your profile, click on the Jobs tab. You'll
see job postings the algorithm thinks match your skills and experience. Read these and tweak your profile to fit jobs you're most
enthusiastic about. If you see a job posting on an organization's
website, you can go to LinkedIn and search for the same job by
key words, titles, or phrases. This should bring up other organizations posting similar positions. Make those bots work for you; train
LinkedIn's algorithm to understand what you're looking for and re-
fine the jobs it shows you. Plug in different attributes such as re-
mote, in office, hybrid, and see whether better opportunities come
up. Track salary information to understand the ranges for positions
in the fields you want.

ACTIVITY/THE FEED

Once you're connected to people with established careers, you'll
see their posts in the Activity section of LinkedIn. When you find
something you like, "like" those posts. Read the comments and
add your own, but keep them short and upbeat, and please proof-

read before you hit Send. Click the "follow" button for companies or influential people in industries of interest to generate more substantive content in your feed. The more research you do within the LinkedIn platform, the more it learns what you're interested in.

Once you've gained confidence, you can share and repost articles from others. The goal is to have people (recruiters, interviewers, your references, your professional idols) nod in agreement, not shake their heads in disbelief.

My friend forwarded the message to me and said, "Is this how young people connect these days and ask for a meeting? Tell me why I shouldn't find this off-putting."

Now, plenty of people wouldn't have been so pissed off by that message. My usually tolerant friend was not among them.

What went wrong?

Well first, there was the salutation calling my friend by her first name. The sender did not know my friend. When you reach out to a stranger, it's best to default to professional and polite. If you don't know someone's honorific (like Professor or Dr.*) or their pronouns (Mr. or Ms.), just default to using their whole name: Dear Rachel Toor, or Hello Rachel Toor. Some people will not be offended if you use only their first name, but why risk being perceived as rude?

Then the tone. My friend had an important job at a famous organization and was not in the habit of going out for coffee in the middle of her workday with some rando she knew nothing about. Plus, this person broke the rule of humility by breezily treating

---

*I'm a professor, but I don't have a doctorate. When someone addresses me as Dr. Toor, I know they haven't spent a lot of time researching me. And while I am married, which is no one's business, I don't use use Mrs. If you must use a title, Ms. or Professor will do.

a stranger like a friend. She is not a friend. She may become one, because, well, that's how my college roommate rolls, but it will take time.

The recent grad did not seem to know anything specific about my friend other than where she worked and that they'd attended the same school. Her *Hey girlfriend!* manner jarred. If she had taken a couple of steps back, kept her personality intact but used a bit more tact, had asked for a quick phone call, had shown she knew my friend had worn more than "quite a few hats" and what they were, had looked harder to see that in fact there were plenty of other graduates of our college in leadership roles at that organization, she would have positioned herself better.

Now, someone else, particularly someone often contacted by young people, might not have felt so annoyed. (This is what happens when people are busy and, frankly, are humans. People have moods, and what works one day won't work on another day or with another person. That's part of what makes this whole thing hard.)

If the young person had shared just a little about herself—that she was deeply involved in community service, that as a woman of color she sought role models in the working world, that she wondered what my friend's experience at an elite college had been like because hers had been tough—the outcome might have been different. On LinkedIn, which my friend never uses, the request might have been okay.

As it was, the message didn't accomplish its purpose.* The way you approach people is what gets them to want to help you. When you reach out to someone you don't know, remember that

*Until she forwarded it to me. At that point I told her yes, this was often the way young people connect these days and she could use it as a teachable moment if she chose. My kind friend invited the young woman to come to her office, explained how she could have done better, and sent her off with some good advice and referrals.

you don't know them. Try to find enough specific information (without coming off as a creeper) to point to areas of connection or shared interest. Default to polite and unassuming.

When I was a young editorial assistant in New York City, I wrote a fan letter to a senior editor at a different publishing house. I admired several books he'd published, and I told him so. He called and invited me to lunch. Every few months, for years, this distinguished man would take me to lunch at the famous Algonquin Hotel where Dorothy Parker presided over the Round Table. I felt like part of a publishing legacy and learned much from him about the industry.

You are building a network. A web. A collection of aunties and uncles. I've responded to every single person who read my book about writing the college application essay. Depending on how they approached me, I've thanked them for the kind words (if they bother to write, their words are always kind), answered specific questions, or gotten interested in them enough to offer to help. One of them is a young woman in Ghana who calls me Auntie Rachel.* I spent time exchanging delightful messages with her on WhatsApp; I spoke to her on Zoom and volunteered to read drafts of her essays. I wanted to do everything I could for that lovely person.

Approach people with humility and eagerness and curiosity, and they will help. I promise. They may even take you to lunch or invite you into their homes for dinner. This kind of outreach, asking strangers to tell you about their jobs and their career paths can, I know, seem stressful and overwhelming. Try to think about it as fun and an investment in your future. Even if you're a giant

---

*I am not her auntie. But there are some cultures and some kids that aren't comfortable calling grown-ups by their first names. I do not like to be addressed formally. I told her to think of me as an auntie in Spokane so she could use an honorific familiar to her.

Practical Pro Tip: List of Contacts

Create a document or spreadsheet, or if you're old school get a notebook, and keep track of every person you've talked to including a recap of the conversation. Writing it all down will help you crystallize and remember what you've learned from them. Make a note of how you found them, their contact info, and any people they've suggested you talk to. Then go back to this document periodically. You'll be surprised at what you've forgotten and notice how many people have given you the same advice.

introvert like me and don't like to talk on the phone (or Zoom), this is a chance to learn about different worlds. Keep that in mind. With these informational meetings, nothing is really at stake. You're not applying for a job (though you are practicing job application skills), and you're getting a ton of free advice. Zoom is a great middle ground between a phone call and a cup of coffee, and many of us have reluctantly come to see it as a good outcome of the COVID pandemic.

Make as many of these approaches as you can. Come up with a good list of questions. And don't forget, there *is* such a thing as a stupid question. If you contact someone on LinkedIn, it would be dumb to ask, "What does your organization do?" That's right on the page. Likewise, don't ask where they went to school or what other jobs they've held. You can look that up.* But you can ask which parts of the organization are successful and which are struggling. You can ask about where they see growth opportunities. You can ask what they're proudest of in their work. You can ask about the work culture—What traditions do they find partic-

---

*The older people get, the more likely they are to omit their year of graduation. We're all afraid of discrimination, and age is one of those factors that catch up with us all.

ularly amusing or meaningful? You can ask about their competitors and what they do well. You can ask what they like and don't like about the job. You can ask what they wish they'd known when they got started in the field. The options are endless.

Again, you're not hitting them up for a job; you just want to learn. It's like all the research you do while writing a term paper that doesn't make it in because it's not relevant. You're on a broad fact-finding mission to deepen your understanding. This is a good time to chuck the teleological perspective that often irritates professors.*

But here's a little inside info that may make this exercise go down more easily. At big organizations, employees often get referral bonuses when they recommend someone who gets hired. If you make a good impression and the person likes you and can see you fitting in, and if there's an opening that's appropriate for you, you could land a job and your connection could get a nice wad of cold hard cash—like thousands of dollars. Everyone wins.

What people say about informational interviews

Max Mankin, who started his own tech company and reports only to a man whose products you probably use every day—and, even if you don't, you know his name because everyone knows his name—says, "Networking and warm intros will get you to an interview much easier than just submitting a resume cold to an open job. But while you're networking, don't be a brown-noser to get intros, and don't gush over people's accomplishments.† It's annoying. Similarly, ask insightful questions and make *specific*,

---

*Please, do not ever ask a teacher, "Do I have to know this? Is this going to be on the test?"

†I'm a gusher. I suspect I've even gushed over Max's achievements, which I know now he finds annoying. Sorry/not sorry, Max.

easily addressable asks. Don't ask questions about things you can find online—don't make them do the work."

Community organizer Sabrina Mauritz says, "When I get calls from people who ask for advice, I am impressed and cultivate those relationships. If you're hungry to get involved, if you are relationship-hungry and are doing the work, I'm ready to fight for you for any job. I'm going to recruit you, and if I can't hire you, I will give you an informal reference. I'll call someone I know or text them and say, 'Hey, I haven't worked closely with this person but I really think they're worth an interview.'"

Here's something that's hard to keep in mind when you're a supplicant: hiring managers are not gatekeepers there to block your access to a dream job. They want to hire people. They want to hire good people, fast. For professional recruiters, the ones you meet at career fairs, it is in fact their job to find people who will be hired. A recruiter's success is determined by whom they hire and how many positions they fill. Make the recruiter's job easier every step of the way.

No one, recruiter or veterinarian or construction manager, likes wading through piles and piles of resumes saying, *No, No, No way, No, OMG no.* They want to fill positions.

Most of us are likely to trust people we know when they make recommendations. This is what makes networking valuable and why making connections is the best way for your application materials to land in an employer's "maybe" or "yes" pile for interviews.

Longtime recruiter Mikki Hubbard says, "The job search is the hardest job you'll ever do and not get paid for it." She says applying for jobs through an organization's career page is like buying a lottery ticket. She says (yes, you've heard this before) it's all about networking. "Any time you can do a face-to-face meeting you get extra points. Meet someone for coffee—everyone should

Practical Pro Tip: Your Personal Board of Directors

Create another document (or keep another notebook) for the folks you'll want to return to for help and advice throughout your career. You've already started creating this board. It may include an older sibling, a best friend, a teacher, your Auntie Rachel, and certain college professors.

You can note their birthdays (so you remember to send cards) or what kind of candy they like (so after someone puts you through a mock interview, you can hand over a giant Kit-Kat). They may change jobs or careers and land at a place you'd like to work. Or they may hear about openings that would be perfect for you. You want them to keep you in mind. Everyone loves to hear success stories, so don't be shy about sharing yours with them.

be able to treat someone to a cup of coffee—and do not hide behind a screen." And don't be afraid to make a telephone call. She adds, "The phone is your friend. Kids don't listen to their voicemail, and they don't like to talk on the phone."*

Don't think *OK, boomer.* Just understand that businesspeople of a certain generation still use the phone. It's fast and efficient. Hubbard says you should learn to leave a decent voicemail message: "It's an opportunity to make a good first impression." This is something you can think about and practice. Make sure you say and spell your name clearly, state the purpose of your call ("Would you be willing to talk to me about your job as an equine acupuncturist, though I know you must be very busy?"), and state your contact information slowly and clearly.

Like most things in life, searching for a job—and finding the right one—involves doing a whole bunch of things that aren't a ton of fun. On the other hand, if you see the process as the be-

---

*You can also ask for a Zoom session.

ginning of a new adventure that could lead, well, who knows where, and approach it with a sense of excitement, enthusiasm, and wonder, you may find it's not such a slog after all. Your world will become bigger and filled with new people who may turn into friends or mentors. We can never have enough of those.

Quick Takes

- Don't overlook your own circle. One of the quickest and easiest ways to network is by leveraging the connections you already have.
- Another gold mine is the Career Services Office at your school. They really are there to help you, so don't hesitate to reach out.
- Exploit LinkedIn for all it's worth.
- When using social media, keep it private or um, "tasteful."
- Do research before contacting someone. Don't ask for a job.
- Show a genuine interest about their experiences in your field of interest and allow the conversation to unfold.
- Talking with strangers can be fun, so don't hide behind a screen. The best connections are developed (and fortified) in person.
- Less texting, more phone calls and semiformal voicemails will go a long way.
- When approaching strangers, default to polite and formal.
- Remember that hiring managers want to hire you.

3 The Job Description

After you've talked to a whole bunch of people, you will have heard about lots of different career paths—jobs you can't believe exist and businesses that allow you to bring your dog to work or give you a subsidy to buy an electric vehicle.

Now you have to apply to work at these cool organizations.

You can look for job postings on industry-specific sites. If you feel most at home on a college campus, universities have staff positions available pretty much all the time. If you're interested in media, there are sites that list jobs in publishing, TV, and film. Professional societies exist for every occupation you can think of, and often they list open positions.

Also, with the connections you've made in your networking effort, once you have a relationship with someone, you can ask about openings in their organization. As I said, some companies offer hefty referral bonuses, so everyone wins if you get hired. A good question to ask early in the process is where the organization advertises and how it typically recruits for entry-level and advanced jobs. Compile a list of resources you've found through your network and a list of those you got through the career center and other places. It helps to be organized. If you don't want to make a spreadsheet, at least create a document to help you keep track of contacts.

Free advice is plentiful

Your family may be eager to give you lots of help, support, and advice, and some of it may be useful. But if they haven't been involved in hiring recently or have worked the same job for years, they may not know about changes in technology that have reshaped the landscape.

If you go to job fairs sponsored by colleges and universities, you'll be exposed to a pack of recruiters, all eager to talk to students about their industries or companies. These tend to be younger folks, enthusiastic and helpful. In fact, recruiting is a great first job for lots of people.

Be polite and professional with everyone you meet. Send thank-you notes. (I'll give you a simple sample later in the book.) Not every recruiter will have a job that's a good match for you, but the world is smaller than you think. Everyone you meet knows other people you might want to meet, and they talk to each other. Recruiters compete for talent, but they also help each other hire good people.

Recently I met a guy in a hotel lobby and asked what he did for work.* He said he'd been a recruiter for Amazon and had recently moved over to Chewy. These are big corporations (well, one is humongous, the other just big), and he hired at an executive level. I asked what was the most common mistake job seekers made. It took him no more than a nanosecond to answer: applying for the wrong job.

At a company like Amazon, tons of jobs are listed and it's easy to hit Submit and upload your resume. Someone like my hotel lobby buddy can see every job you've applied for at their organization. It's like throwing a handful of undercooked spaghetti at the wall. Nothing sticks and you've made a big mess. He clicks No

---

*Yes, I talk to strangers. As I said, I'm professionally nosy.

on all those applications, and those folks get a little red mark by their name. Not good.

You must tailor your materials—your cover letter and your resume—to each job. Glenn Gutmacher says, "One version of the resume does not fit all. If you're applying to ten different jobs, you should have ten different resumes. Using the same version of your resume for every job is just stupid." He continues, "Employers want to see effort. Everyone has discretionary effort. The ones who go the extra mile get noticed. Those are the people that make an impression. Opportunities go to people who put in the extra effort."

That means you need to treat the job search as a job. Research, research, research. Apply your skills and grit just as you did in classes.

I hope you haven't already learned this the hard way. It's easy to get discouraged when you think about the amount of effort required. So don't just work harder, work smarter. When I gave a workshop for a group of current students and talked about this and about how you need to keep the bots from trashing your application, a cartoon lightbulb went on over one young woman's head.

A few years before, she had applied for a job at Barnes and Noble, and minutes after she clicked Submit, she got a thanks-but-no-thanks letter. How could they have read it so quickly?

Well, I said, she was turned down by R2-D2, who can read astonishingly fast, being a robot and all, and who may have made sad little squeals while he incinerated her resume.

Her mistake was likely an obvious one. She didn't match what she submitted to the job description. And I mean *match*. You have to know what they're looking for and tell them in language robots understand. Glenn Gutmacher warns that "program management" and "project management" won't come up as the same thing. Incorporate the organization's language. Phrase it the way they phrase it. If one job asks for "impeccable customer support skills," list that. If another wants "customer support experience," that's what you should have on your resume. You need to be that specific to get past the bots. For each job, make sure your materials exactly match the description. That means you've got to do word searches.

While you might like me to give you a list of keywords to include on your materials, and even to tell you exactly what percentage of your one-page resume and cover letter should be devoted to them, it's just not that simple. Instead, I suggest you google things like "how to beat the AI bots in a job search." You'll find tons of information far more detailed than what I can provide here. This book is meant to help you with the mindset needed to be successful and the awareness of how the process generally works; the specifics will vary by industry, organization, and manager. And not all organizations use automated tracking systems, though most big companies do. You can get plenty of information about those that do from your college career center.

Since a big mistake many people make is to apply for the wrong job, you need to learn how to read a job description. These documents are often the work of committees, and every word has been carefully chosen or argued about. Then they get vetted by human resources experts to make sure they're, well, legal and not discriminatory. It's in your interest to study these and understand exactly what they say they're looking for. Then tailor your materials to fit their needs. Remember, it's not about what you want, it's how you can contribute.

Job title

Start with the title. It may seem straightforward, but each job differs, and so does each organization. "Administrative assistant" can mean you screen calls, schedule meetings, and pick up dry cleaning. (I hope it doesn't mean picking up dry cleaning, but you never know.) Or it can mean sitting in on all sorts of high-level meetings, taking notes, and being privy to a lot of sensitive information. Much depends on who you'll be working for, the culture of the organization, and how your supervisor sees the role.* So it would be a mistake to think the job title tells you everything you need to know. "Project manager" might be different from "project coordinator." You need to look for the details.

Things get more complicated when job titles are quirkier. Some organizations have gotten, um, creative in their titles. Most job listings for "warriors" or "heroes" are in health care, particularly nursing. "Evangelist" jobs are generally not in religion but in techie "product evangelism," which likely just means sales. You'll see "growth hackers" wanted for marketing positions, and educational and training companies look for "ninjas." About 20 percent of ads that contain "champion" and "rock star" in the title are, I'm sorry to say, not in sports or music but are for the hospitality industry.

These ads tell you something about how the organization sees itself. This is a good time to think about the match. Do you want to be with a bunch of folks who come to work ready to play, or will you be happier in a more formal environment?

Description of the job responsibilities

Next you'll need to read the summary description. This is the big picture of what the job is—why does this job exist? It can be short: "Plan, direct, or coordinate investment strategy or operations for a large pool of liquid assets supplied by institutional investors or

---

*If you're lucky, you'll find a boss who is interested in mentoring you.

individual investors." Or "Edit moving images on film, video, or other media. May work with a producer or director to organize images for final production. May edit or synchronize soundtracks with images." Or much longer:

Social Media Assistant (Full-Time Temporary)
Thingy is hiring a New York- or Los Angeles-based Social Media Assistant to help maintain and expand the brand's suite of social media accounts. This role requires a social media-savvy individual with sharp writing skills, knowledge of the Film and TV industries and related trends, and a keen visual eye.

You will be responsible for assisting the Senior Social Media Manager in supporting Thingy on Facebook, X, Instagram, LinkedIn, and other channels. You'll pitch creative ideas for interactive social initiatives and story promotion and pick up news stories in real time to share on social media. Basic graphic design skills are a major plus, as you will assist in creating images for the site and social feeds.

The ideal candidate is a self-starter who can quickly learn the tone and flavor of the Thingy brand and has a deep understanding of how to translate stories to social networks. Key to your success is consuming social media with an eye toward tracking entertainment trends, paired with the ability to recognize when a swell in online chatter could point to the opportunity for a story.

I've underlined key words that might be good to use in your resume and cover letter. I suggest you underline or highlight such words for every job you want to apply for and customize your materials to use exactly these words and phrases. You need to do this so you're not screened out by artificial intelligence.

This description tells you the person in this role is responsible for the company's accounts on various social media sites, which means you need to understand how different sites are used, the personality of each, and the audiences targeted by those accounts. If a job interests you because you've done something similar, in your cover letter and resume you'll need to speak to the specifics of what you accomplished. You can say, "I have a keen visual eye . . ." then describe how you used photos and videos to double your student organization's Insta following from five hundred to a thousand in six months.*

You don't want to say, "I'm creative and have lots of ideas for how to interact with others on social media." Instead, give specific instances of things you've done. You might write, "When a bunch of beagles were rescued from a testing lab, I started a trend that swept through campus, with 150 students making TikToks of their favorite freedom songs. I used these responses as part of an advertising campaign for a Save Snoopy event that raised $5,000 for a local animal shelter."

And throw in some evidence you know how to use social media to speak to different audiences. Maybe you are social media coordinator for your sorority, but you also handled socials for a coffee shop and worked on a multi-platform media plan for a local pharmaceutical company in a marketing class. How many followers did you accumulate? How did you attract them? As we'll see in later chapters, in your written materials you can explain how you developed different voices for posts from each of these organizations. The job description gives you all the clues you need to show (not tell) what you've done and point out how that is directly relevant to the position.

You *must* use the same language as the job description. If they want a "social media creator," write that instead of "social media coordinator." If they require competence in Microsoft Power-

---

*Quantify as much as you can.

Point, don't list Prezi. You'll still use your own voice, but you'll need to repeat back to them certain words the gatekeeping robot wants to hear. Otherwise he will incinerate your resume.

Organization description

Next, there may be an organization description. This is where you start your research. After you see how they describe themselves, you'll need to do a deep dive into what others say about them. And I mean deep. Please don't apply if you know nothing more than what you read in the short "about us" description.

Now, for a job like the one at Thingy, you may think: *Great! Social media is something I know how to do. I have 2,000 followers on the Gram. I'm active on all of these channels. And ideas? Boy, do I have ideas!*

The most important thing I see when I read this ad is: "Can quickly learn the tone and flavor of the Thingy brand." What you do on your own social accounts means zip. You may be one of the lucky few who gets paid to post photos of your dog, but when you work for someone else you have to understand the tone and flavor of their brand. That means you need to read as much about Thingy as you can. What language do they use? What is the culture of their business? Your voice and your taste don't matter; you will have to learn to mimic theirs.

And they'll be looking for someone with good judgment. One ill-advised post can land a company in the *New York Times*, and not in a good way. While there's a saying that all publicity is good publicity, it's not really true, especially when it comes to the mistakes organizations make on social media. If you've gotten your employer press for being racist, sexist, or homophobic, or for trashing the competition and starting an electronic war, you might soon be looking for another job.

For each job application, your task is to understand the organization. You may think because you've gone to college, you'd be a good candidate to do social media for a university. But the way students talk is different from the kinds of professional communications written by each department. You've seen the university from only one perspective, a small slice of a complex ecosystem that has many missions and goals. You may talk about sports with your friends, but a university's communications manager will use the word "athletics." No undergraduate admissions office ever "rejects" a student. They "deny" an application. You'd have to understand this difference if you wanted to become an admissions officer.

Moving beyond the ad, you'll need to look at the company's website to find its stated mission and values. When I talked to Cheryl Chamberlain, chief administrative officer at McKinstry, a big building and energy services company, she explained that while they do build heating and cooling systems, its leaders care most about sustainability. If you look at the McKinstry website, there's a section called "What We Do." You can click on government, health care, biomass, and hospitality and learn what the organization cares about. The company is building buildings, sure, but its "Who We Are" page contains its core values—outlining its vision, mission, and commitment to people and partnerships.

Now, not every construction management major will care about all this stuff. That doesn't mean they wouldn't be happy working at a company like McKinstry. What matters is the match. Making sure you and the company are compatible. While job hunting is practical—you have to feed yourself, buy gas, and think about repaying student loans before you get buried under compounding interest—you also want to work at a place that aligns with your interests or, at the very least, doesn't compromise your values. This is important for your long-term well-being. Another consideration is whether the job will help you develop skills and experiences to make you more valuable to other employers down the career line.

The best way to understand an organization's culture is to talk to current employees. Before you send in an application, try to get in touch with as many current (and former) employees as you can. LinkedIn will help. You can send a message saying you're interested in applying for a job at McKinstry or Thingy or Dog Stylists USA and you would be grateful to hear about their experience.*

Sites like Glassdoor allow people to write reviews of their workplaces. Those can be useful, but first spend a minute thinking about anonymous online reviews. You know they're most often written by people who are pissed off. How many times have you been disappointed by a product or a service and written or posted a complaint? I'll bet it's more often than you've posted that someone at the organization went out of their way to help you, or you were delighted by something you bought.

Research, research, research

Most people don't spend enough time thinking about the places they're applying to. One of your main tasks in the job search is doing research. A ton of it. You are an investigative reporter, a cultural anthropologist, a snooper. You want to find all the good things and as much of the dirt as you can and sift through to know if it will be a good match and then to be hired.

What you don't want is to learn all that stuff too late. Like when you're in the interview and someone asks, as they will—*Why do you want to work here?*

---

*This is not an opportunity for you to sell yourself to them. You are seeking information. It's not about you, it's about them. When you're talking, you're not learning.

When they say *here*, they don't mean in this field, or this industry, or this part of the world. They mean *at this very organization*. Here means *here*. Your answer must be filled with specifics. Before you submit any materials, make sure you know the answer to that question. It can't be "Because I need a job." Or "I'm desperate for money." Or "I need to move out of my parents' basement." Or "I think it will give me a boost to a different position." Or "I can't think of anything else, and this fits in with my major." Those may all be true. But if you can't come up with good reasons you want to work *here*, you need to keep looking.

Something you should have learned in college (but may not have) is how to check sources. What an organization says about itself may not reveal biases. If you're concerned with, say, the health impact of sugar, you may have found jobs listed at two organizations: the International Life Sciences Institute and the Partnership for a Healthier America. When you look at their websites, you'll see they're both nonprofits that seem to do work you might like to support. But if you dig in—even do a quick Wikipedia search—you'll find the ILSI is funded by companies like McDonalds, Pepsi, and other food industry giants. So know before you go, and make sure you understand as much as you can about the place and its values so you end up in a good situation.

Internships

If you're reading this book while you're still in college, here's some good news. One of the best pieces of advice hiring managers have to offer is that you should get an internship during school. (If you didn't, it's fine. You can get other "real world" experiences that can demonstrate your passion and show how things you've learned will be useful to employers—see the next section on volunteering.) You can use your career center to find out what's available and get help in applying.

The bad news? It's competitive, especially for high-demand fields like finance, where the chances of being hired are similar to the odds of getting into Harvard or Stanford—single digit acceptances from thousands of applicants. An internship is one of the best ways to experience work in the real world, with a lot less pressure. It's a good way station between the mindset poles created by loving family and professors (*It's all about you*) and the cold, hard world of work (*I don't care about you; what can you do for me?*). Internships not only provide a taste of what work can look like after graduation but immerse you in an environment that may be a bit foreign. And applying for internships requires the same skill set as job seeking and is great practice. Even more important, internships may help you identify the kind of work you want to do. Or not want to do, ever again.

Volunteering

In college, you may have felt overwhelmed with schoolwork and keeping fit and, well, socializing, but you still might have been able to squeeze out a few hours to volunteer for something. And once you've graduated and are in job-search mode, you want something to keep you busy. If you can't get an established internship, you could still volunteer for an organization you care about. This is also an excellent opportunity to get in the door. Once you're there and a position opens up, you'll already be in place.

This is a way many of us started out. I took a seminar first semester of senior year with an editor from Oxford University Press. She asked what I was planning to do after graduation. I said I wanted to work on a dude ranch out west (having never been out west or on a dude ranch).

"Why don't you try publishing," she asked.

So spring semester I commuted from New Haven to New York City each Friday of my senior year in college to type letters for a different editor at Oxford. I wasn't paid, and the train fare stretched my budget, but I was fortunate to be able to crash with relatives for the weekends. After graduation, a full-time editorial assistant position opened up working for the editor who'd taught me. I was hired. She became a mentor and has remained a friend ever since.*

Lise Chapman, who worked in finance for many years and is now an educational and career counselor, started the 1stGenYale organization to support FGLI (first-gen low-income) students and alumni. She says, "Many people end up with jobs they truly like because they started as a volunteer." Whether it's collecting names on a petition or cleaning stalls at a therapeutic riding facility, you don't know what such an opportunity could lead to and what connections you might make.

Requirements/qualifications

Hiring managers have told me people should apply for jobs they are 40 percent qualified for. If you think you're interested, do your best to show how equivalent experience might substitute for requirements. You may not know which keywords the automated tracking system will have been programmed to know are essential. You might say that while you don't have a BA degree yet, you will graduate in May. Or you are planning to learn Python over the summer.

Mike Bergmann had been a research director at a semiconductor company and hired many scientists and engineers at all

*And twenty-nine years after graduation, I got to try being a wrangler for eight days at a guest (I learned not to say "dude") ranch in Montana. It was even better than I'd imagined.

levels. He didn't have his human resources office screen applicants. "I wanted to see everyone," he says. "No insult to the HR department, but screening resumes is a nuanced activity. Hiring managers know best what they are looking for; I didn't want to miss someone with great potential because they got screened out for not having some item listed on the job requirements. It only takes a minute to scan a resume, and for the large investment being made in hiring someone, I have a minute to glance at anyone's resume who made the effort to apply."

That means while the job description may say a BS degree is required, or even a BS in engineering, Mike didn't care. Seriously. He just didn't care. Ivy League school? Community college? Didn't matter. He'd look at a resume and decide if it was worth a ten-minute phone call to see how an applicant thought and how eager they were. He hired engineers without degrees.

A scholarly book editor I know never graduated from college. You can bet that when he applied, the job description said a degree was required. He was able to make a good case for himself based on his years of experience working at one of the best bookstores in the country. Over a long and storied career as an editor, he has published many pathbreaking works of academic research.

Most jobs will ask for some related experience for a range of years. You can make the case that while you don't have direct experience doing exactly that role, you've used the same skills in internships, summer jobs, and even hobbies. Rebuilding a car, for example, might show the aptitude for mechanical work needed in an engineering job. Moderating a Facebook group with 140,000 members is impressive experience. Translate that background into what the role requires, and you'll be in good shape. Maybe you've invested your bat mitzvah money and turned $500 into $25,000. If you can show how you did that, an investment bank recruiter might be convinced you're that company's kind of person.

Many jobs are about relationships. Some health care work can depend more heavily on customer service skills than on specialized knowledge. How well do you handle being around people? Babysitting or creating latte art at a drive-through coffee stand may be a way to show years of experience if you can articulate clearly how those experiences relate directly to what the job description says is required.

Here's something to consider. Tom Feulner, who recruited for Yelp, says many of the people who applied for jobs they weren't entirely qualified for tended to come from the same demographic: white men. He says people of color who had far more impressive credentials, when asked why they didn't apply for certain jobs, said they didn't think they met the criteria. According to the Pew Research Center, there continues to be a gender gap in wages. In 2020, women earned 84 percent of what men did. Don't be arrogant, but don't be afraid to try for things that might seem out of reach. Go for it.

Certifications

Mikki Hubbard, a longtime recruiter in Atlanta, says many college students use Apple computers, but most big organizations use Microsoft products on PCs. She says digital natives should be great at Excel or Tableau. What sort of instant messaging tools do you know? Have you used Slack? Have you videoconferenced only on Zoom? Before you contact someone for an informational chat or you're contacted for a job interview, make sure you've practiced using Microsoft Teams and Google Meet and whatever the most recent platform is. These have features that are similar but different. Learn as many of them as you can. Do a practice session with someone you know before you chat with a stranger.

One way to prove you know the programs you want to list on

your resume is through professional certifications. These are critical in technical fields. Company websites list certifications they require. You can do online tests and list the certifications on your resume and on your LinkedIn profile. As you network, you can ask professionals in each field which certifications would be most useful. If you want to write video games, you might want to invest in learning C++, Java, or Python.*

Here's an embarrassing confession. While researching this book, I asked the helpful bots at LinkedIn to suggest writing jobs for me based on my current work profile. That includes a dozen years in publishing, being the author of seven books, and currently being a professor of creative writing. LinkedIn spit out some jobs for me and gave me a list of how many of the required skills I had (based on the information I'd provided in my profile). Yikes! At best I had about four out of fifteen. This is because I had done a terrible job writing my LinkedIn profile. Some of the jobs said I needed to know Microsoft Word.

Well, then. If I know how to do anything on a computer, it's word processing. I saw I could take a free test to get certified in Word. Great! I love challenges, and who doesn't like getting things for free? So I went through the fifteen questions on the test. They were much harder than I expected, and I got a score of 40 percent. Big ding to my fragile ego. There were tons of Word functions I'd never needed and so never bothered to learn. If I'd been applying for a job where Word was required, I'd have needed to invest a couple of hours to watch free video tutorials. I want to believe I would have learned a bunch of things and then been able to pass the test and get the certification. If I failed again, I'd study more and retake the test.

When an organization says you need to know PowerPoint or

---

*Please don't take my word for it. Ask someone who writes these things.

Adobe Illustrator or Python, it's in your interest to make sure you really know these programs and can prove it. At the very least, specify your level of accomplishment—novice, intermediate, expert—on your resume where you list these skills and include this information on your LinkedIn profile. Don't exaggerate, because an exam could be in your future.

Everyone says they know how to proofread. But if you've taken tests that show you know the difference between an em dash and an en dash and which to use when,* that will put you ahead of all those who've only done favors for their friends by looking over college papers. Once you get further in the application process, you're likely to be asked to take tests and do projects specific to the organization and the role. But first, you must get past the initial screening. Even if the organization isn't big enough to use an automated tracking system, a human reading your materials will choose applicants who make it easy for them to say yes.

Here's an important point about putting proficiencies, especially language skills, on your resume. If you list a language, mention your level of fluency and be prepared for someone at the organization to test whether you accurately described your abilities. If you say you're fluent in Cantonese, don't be surprised if someone raised in Guangzhou is asked to join the meeting or be on a call with you. For this reason, you *must* accurately represent your fluency or level of any skills listed on your resume.

Some certifications† cost money. If you have a student account on LinkedIn, you can get these free. Many public libraries have agreements with companies that offer online courses and certifi-

---

*Even if you're not applying for those jobs, it's still good to know the difference between the dashes.

†Universities often offer "certificate programs" that act like minors. Make sure you find out if these are nationally recognized. Not all certificates are meaningful to those outside the campus walls.

cations at no cost.* And check with people in your network, your professors, and the career center to see which certifications are valued for various paths in an industry that interests you. Some may not be worth the money. But if you choose certifications carefully, that can be a good way to invest in your future.

Remember, the job search won't be a breeze. You'll need to put in work and make some sacrifices. In the often icky world of being a grown-up, you have to channel that geriatric rock and roll band and realize you can't always get what you want. But if you try sometime, you'll find you get what you need. You may need certifications.

Salary

In a later chapter I'll go into how and why you should negotiate once you get an offer, but you may not end up with the whopping salary you think you deserve, at least initially. I've often heard college students, when asked their plans for after graduation, say, "I'll nail some high-paying job, work for a year, and then take time off to travel."

Yup, sounds great. But I think they underestimate how many other people apply for those high-paying jobs and overestimate their chances of actually landing one. You're probably in better shape if you've just graduated from an elite university in a high-demand major. But remember, lots of other people graduate from elite universities with those same majors. And many have done internships or worked summer jobs that give them direct experience, or they've networked their little Zoom faces off to be referred by people they've won over.

---

* As soon as you graduate from college, or even before, get a public library card. It will give you access to a world of resources, including librarians, the most helpful people in the world.

With few exceptions, recent college grads are not in a position to make big salary demands, despite applicants' hopes and dreams. If pulling in a lot of dough right after college is important to you, majoring in something like art history may not have been the way to go.* Consulting firms often hire philosophy majors or physicists because they are trained to think rigorously and they like doing hard things. It's less about specific skills than about the ability to reason through a problem. So pursue study in subjects that interest you—really, the world needs more philosophy majors—but also, maybe learn how to code.

Some jobs will list salary ranges and others won't, though some states are now requiring employers to be transparent about what they pay. Also, some benefits that may not be of interest to you right now, like health insurance and employer contributions to a retirement plan, can add up and make a salary that isn't as big much more valuable. It will be up to you to do research. Again, tools available to you through your college career center can be a huge help. Take some time to learn to put together a budget. Before you apply for jobs, research the cost of housing. You want to know enough in advance to be able to move quickly when you get a job offer. It would stink to accept a job you want, then put together your budget and discover you can't afford to take that job.

While you may not be in a great position to negotiate when you're headed into a first job, doing good work can be the path to success. It's a lot easier to be promoted from within, especially at a big organization, than it is to get in the door. Once I started working at Oxford University Press, I moved up the ladder to being an editor very quickly. Not because I was so great, though I always stayed late and asked a lot of questions, but because I had the support of a powerful boss.

---

*Studies have shown that over time after graduation, the wage gap between STEM and humanities degrees decreases significantly.

The aboutness of the job

The main thing is to suss out what the job is really about. What do I mean by that when I've just given examples of job descriptions? Well, here's a way to think of it. A good piece of art uses something as a topic. Let's take a movie as an example, say, *The Wizard of Oz*. In one sense, the movie is about a girl and her little dog who get caught up in a tornado and blown to a distant place with kind people made of straw and tin and scary flying monkeys and green-faced bitches—I mean witches. A quintet* of weirdos go on a journey to get help from a wizard for things they think they need but already have, and they encounter all sorts of obstacles along the way. That's the situation.

But what the movie is about—its aboutness, I'd call it—is that, well, there's no place like home. It's about learning to appreciate where you live and the people who love you. It's also a classic version of the hero's journey, the plot of every epic from ancient Greece's *Odyssey*, to China's *Journey to the West*, to George Lucas's *Star Wars*, to baseball. All of these are about facing challenges in a quest to get back home.

So, while the job description will tell you the situation, it won't give you the aboutness of the work. A job at the library isn't about sorting books, it's about customer service. It's about helping people who need shelter and protection. A job in a lab isn't about conducting cool experiments, it's about being part of a team that patiently washes beakers to get something done. Working on a ranch isn't about playing cowgirl, it's about keeping animals safe.

To apply for the right job—one you're sort of qualified for and will enjoy doing—you must know what it's about. You can learn how to decode a job description, but the best way to understand

---

*Don't count out Toto.

Practical Pro Tip: Word Clouds

For each job description, list all the words that seem important. Check your resume and cover letter to make sure you include and use them in exactly the same way. Perhaps the easiest way to do this is by using a word cloud generator. Use one of the free apps to paste in the job description. It will show you which words the organization is stressing. Your materials should duplicate that.

what a job is really like and what a successful candidate will look like is by talking to people who are doing that work.

Check in with your peers

Remember what I said about networking? It's essential. When you're researching, look for people who are currently doing the job you want to apply for—at that specific organization or at others. Ask about their experiences. What do they like best about their work? What tasks do they have to slog through to get to the fun stuff? What has surprised them in their work? What do they wish they'd asked in the interview? What other jobs did they consider? Ask for examples that show the company culture.

Remember when I said people love to help? And that everyone likes to talk about themselves and be thought of as an expert? That's especially true for those who are at the beginning of their careers and aren't yet tired and jaded. Think of every college tour you took when you were in high school. Those backward-walking tour guides were thrilled to share their experiences and expertise, even if they'd only been on campus for a few weeks.

Peer-to-peer networks can be invaluable. Treat everyone, including those your own age, with respect. Remember, when you're talking, you're not learning. They may want to get to know

Practical Pro Tip: Create a Job-Search Study Group

Smart students in tough classes often form study groups. Some professors even require students to work together to learn concepts and do projects. Group work is an essential part of the real world.

Create a study group focused on career development with your like-minded peers. Read and comment on each other's resumes and cover letters. We all need editors all the time. Create a shared document where each of you can list questions you were asked during interviews. Create a shared spreadsheet with a list of businesses that have recruited students from your school for internships and jobs. Include names and contact information, and maybe one of the people from one of those companies will want to speak to your group when they get wind of what you've done. Make sure you're all connected on LinkedIn, and use each other's connections to expand your network.

you, and you may become friends with them. That would be wonderful. But at this point you're asking them for a favor, even if it seems like something they'll enjoy doing.

Try to avoid the tendency we all have to prove we're smart and capable and cover up insecurities by bragging. It's way more attractive to find someone who says, "I don't really know what I'm doing, and I need help. Can you help me?" Even if you're smart and capable—and I believe you are—you don't need to broadcast that when you're asking for a favor. Just ask good questions.*
Remember, when I use the word "smart" as a key ingredient in a successful job applicant, I really mean curious. Hiring managers have all told me they want someone who really wants to learn.

---

*Remember, there *is* such a thing as a stupid question, and you shouldn't ask it. Often those questions aren't really questions but are in fact statements.

That goes for talking to peers. I know it's hard to seem naive. But if you've never done something before—like a specific job at a specific organization—the fact is you're ignorant as all get-out. Own that. No one will judge you for it.

Quick Takes

- Most people like to be asked for help.
- Recruiters can be very useful—even if you're not looking for a job in their industry.
- Be nice to everyone.
- Tailor your materials to every single job.
- Match job descriptions exactly, or you will immediately be screened out by robots.
- Apply for the right job—don't spam a company with your resume.
- Don't underestimate what you bring. Don't be cocky, but if you tend to doubt yourself, think about whether that's a result of being a member of a group that isn't entitled. As I tell brilliant and talented women and BIPOC, "I need you to channel the confidence of a mediocre white man."
- Think about what you can contribute, not what you want.
- Much depends on the person who will be your direct manager.
- Be prepared to say why you want to work at this organization—you will be asked.
- It may be worthwhile to get certified in programs you think you know.
- Make sure you know what the job is really about.
- Talk to people who are currently doing the job.

4 *A Few Words about "Match"*

As in dating, so with the job search—one person's right swipe is another's *hell no!*

You can like a person's photos and think they've written a snappy, funny self-description, and you have oh so many hobbies and interests in common (He likes rats! She also thinks avocado and kale hired the same PR firm! Yes, Cheez-Its are the best snack!), but then you're sitting next to him at a bar and, well, people across the room can hear him chugging his beer and he keeps checking his reflection in the window and he smells like your grandpa. Ugh. Just not the right person for you.

With jobs it can also be that simple. Does it feel like you could match? For most jobs straight from college, there are a lot of applicants with similar qualifications and interests. There are lots of jobs in the same industry. Some people will match more closely with a specific organization's culture than others.

Match is a two-way street

You must do a whole lot of research *before* applying, and while there are clear mistakes you can make (you're reading this book so you can avoid them), if you don't get a certain job, it may not be because you're not qualified but because they found someone who seemed like a better match. You can't take everything personally or you'll become sad and discouraged. That's not a good look when applying for jobs (even though the process can be disheartening).

Remember what I said early on: It's no longer all about you. It's about how you can contribute to the organization. Each organization has a unique culture, and while it's true that once you're there you can do your part to make it even better, you won't be successful if you think they will adapt to you. Hear this: It's up to you to discover a good match.

That means figuring out who you are, being clear about your values, and knowing what you care about. That's important not just for understanding what kind of job you want, but for knowing where you want to do it. You can be a copywriter at any number of places: a conservative Christian book publisher, a super-hip progressive advertising agency, a firm that provides documents to set up LLCs. Companies need website content for dog food, or boutique hotels, or genetic testing kits. Each of those industries cultivates a unique culture, and each firm will have its own flavor.

You're looking for a job because, presumably, you need to make money and you want to start a career. A job—any job—is not about fulfilling your social needs. However, you're likely to be spending more time at work than having romantic dinners or hanging out with friends. If you're not happy in the workplace or feel you must hide important aspects of yourself, well, no job is worth that. If you're at the right place, it may result in friendships that last long after you leave the organization.

It's in everyone's interest to find a good match. There are as many dysfunctional organizations as there are dysfunctional families. And it doesn't take much for one person to create a toxic environment. Think about the worst class you ever took, or a bad experience on a group trip, or even a family reunion that turned

Practical Pro Tip: Questions to Ask Yourself

Think about (and maybe even write out) answers to some basic questions.

What kinds of problems do you want to solve in your work? Do you want to work with organizations that focus on climate change, social justice issues, housing issues, food-related issues, making fashionable/sustainable clothing/packaging/cars?

Do you want to work on the problems directly—doing the science, writing the code, passing the laws, building the houses, growing/distributing the food, designing the clothes—or are you the person who will explain these things to others to raise money or raise awareness or get the legislators interested?

Do you like to work with kids, older people, peers, or mixed groups?

Would you prefer to be "customer facing" or behind the scenes?

Do you work best by yourself or in groups? Are you a group leader or a team player?

Do you like to do things with your hands or with words/images?

Is making money—no matter what you're doing—the most important thing? How long can you work at a place whose values are not aligned with your own?

out to be a freaking disaster. Often one person's behavior can sour the experience for many. Sometimes one person can create a situation where everyone else bands together against them. You don't want to be that lone person. And you don't want to be in a situation like that. Hiring managers are generally aware of their organization's culture and have an idea of who will fit in.

Cheryl Chamberlain, the chief administrative officer at McKinstry, the building company, was clear when I asked her about the biggest mistake applicants make. She said, "People do the classic preparation. They think about the job, what they would be doing, who the job serves, who the job impacts. Then they think separately about their strengths. What skills do they have, what are their preferences?" She pointed out most people stay at jobs two to four years, then start the whole process again.

But, she adds, often they never think about the most important step. She asks herself, "Has this person spent energy thinking what they're really passionate about? What are the values that drive them?"

"Most importantly," she says, "what do they think their purpose is in life? What direction are they trying to follow?"

Your authentic interest is what sets you apart from every other applicant—how you and that organization align. You don't just want a job, any job.* You want the right job at the right place.

Lise Chapman, founder of 1stGenYale, says she asks students what they do in their spare time. If they say, "I love to build model airplanes" but think their destiny is to be a doctor, they might try to find a way to tie their hobby to a career interest. Maybe that's in biomedical engineering. Or in construction. "Where are you the happiest? That's where your career journey should begin. Go to what you like to do," advises Chapman.

And being happy means being comfortable. Don't try to contort yourself into someone you're not. You are who you are, talk the way you talk, wear what you wear, and have a personality many people find appealing. An introvert in a job that requires cold-calling potential customers will be as miserable as the life of the party extrovert forced to sit alone in a cubicle.

---

*I know you think you just want any job and you're a bit panicky and desperate, and you may have already been rejected by the bots because you applied for jobs before reading this book. But I'm encouraging you to be more thoughtful and deliberate as you approach the process instead of throwing undercooked spaghetti against the wall.

Practical Pro Tip: The Previous Employee

Asking about the person who held the position before can be tricky, but you can also get useful information that way. In the interview, you ask whether this is a new position, created because of business growth or reorganization, or whether someone was promoted from the role or moved elsewhere in the organization. You can then tell from the answer if the person has left the organization, and if so, if on good or bad terms. Focus on collecting information (and possible red flags), but be careful about asking too directly.

In some circumstances you may want to try to locate and reach out to the person who previously had the job—before you apply. It's often not that hard to figure out from LinkedIn. Or see if you can find someone else at the company who will talk to you generally about the culture and the job, then, if you do make a good bond with them, ask if they know why the position is open. It could be due to a reorganization or an internal promotion, or just a bad match.

No one can thrive in an environment where they feel uncomfortable. While every job requires professionalism, no job is worth compromising your sense of self.

Employers have had to adapt to changes in the cultural climate, and laws protect certain classes of people from discriminatory behavior. But microaggressions abound in many places. If in the hiring process something sets off your personal alarms, pay attention. Talk over those things with your network. Not all employers are good interviewers, and not all bosses are people you'll be happy working for. While I've said it's not all about you and what you want, in the most important sense of course it's about you. You'll spend many hours at work. You don't want to feel alienated from the beginning. When you're interviewing, you can inquire about the person who previously held the position you're applying for and ask where they are now.

In this book I've chosen to use "match" instead of the more common "fit" when I address finding the right workplace. That's because "fit" and "culture fit" can serve as a form of discrimination—the basis of the "old boys club" hiring that has persisted throughout history and served to keep out people who looked or thought differently.

You can get a sense of an organization by scouring websites and scanning the photos of those in leadership positions. How many of them look like you? Look at the names in the staff directory. Google people or find them on LinkedIn. You'll learn a lot. Then ask questions about anything that concerns you. What is their commitment to ensuring a diverse workforce? How long do people usually stay?

More progressive employers, instead of mentioning "fit," will talk instead about candidates who have useful qualifications and share the organization's goals and values. As with dating, the main idea is to find a match where you can grow and feel comfortable being who you are. And even, believe it or not, have some fun.

Quick Takes

- Remember that although you don't have to be your whole self at work, you don't want to feel alienated if your values don't align with those of the organization.
- Don't become so desperate to get a job that you end up in a place that makes you uncomfortable.
- Spend time thinking about your values—even make a list of what things you believe are most important—then check that against an organization's mission statement.

- Think about what makes you happy and which interests you'd most like to pursue. Those might make great career choices.
- Ask (tactfully) about the person who had the job you're applying for and possibly reach out to them.

5 *The Cover Letter*

Send a cover letter whether or not it's required

There are two main written parts of the application process: the cover letter and the resume. They are not the same thing. In this chapter, I'll focus on the letter.

Not all jobs require cover letters. You can imagine which kinds of industries care about them (anything that involves written communication, like law, publishing, marketing) and those that don't (science and tech).

However, even if a cover letter isn't required, it can be in your interest to include one. Especially if it's good. If you haven't gotten the message by now, let me say it again. Most recent grads, and in fact many people who have worked for decades, aren't great at this process.

It will sound like extra work, and it is. But it's also essential. And, again, you need to tailor your cover letter and your resume for each job. A good cover letter will show who you are and tell how you might be able to contribute to a particular organization in a specific role. Its purpose is to get the recipient to want to have a conversation with you. The two documents, cover letter and resume, don't repeat the same information but work together to create a fuller picture of you.

In the cover letter, you can make a case for yourself even if the required qualifications don't make you an obvious choice. Don't lie. Don't exaggerate. But do use the keywords in the job description. If the job requires you to be proficient in Excel, you can say, "while I don't yet have a certificate in Excel, I plan to teach myself the program over the summer." That might help you not get screened out by the bots. And for the human eventually reading the letter, you can explain that the low GPA listed on your resume* is the result of your having worked thirty-six hours a week on the graveyard shift driving the airport shuttle bus and taking an overload of classes so you could graduate in three years without student loans because you are supporting three younger siblings.

The cover letter is a place for you to convey your enthusiasm, interests, and commitment.† And it's an opportunity for you to make the person receiving it feel valued and to convey that you understand what the mission of the organization is and how you can contribute.

If you're exhausted or demoralized or trying to apply to as many jobs as you can, noticing that a cover letter is not required may fill you with delight. Instead, see a cover letter as an opportunity. Recruiter Wenda Cenexant says, "Not enough people use them. They make it easier to get a picture of who you are. If they're not required, people should send them anyway. Fifteen people out of a hundred send a cover letter. That puts you in a top tier of applicants."

Library supervisor Caitlin Wheeler says the jobs she hires for do not require cover letters, but if someone sends one, she will read it: "I value them as a way to get to know the individual." And even though she studied creative writing in graduate school, she knows not everyone has done so. "Just because you're not a good writer doesn't mean you're not going to be good at the job,"

---

*Not all jobs require you to list your GPA—this varies by industry. But if you graduate with honors, by all means mention that.

†Though just including those words will not be sufficient. Keep reading.

she says. Of course, it helps to write clearly and concisely and to sound like yourself—the best, smartest version of yourself. (More on that in my last little chapter.)

Mike Bergmann, who hires scientists and engineers, says he seldom reads cover letters. Many employers I've talked to, especially those in technical fields or ones who are looking for very specific experiences and skills, say the same thing. Mike says he'll scan the resume, and if someone seems promising, he'll call the person for a half-hour chat. He knows how to cut through fluff and get what he needs to know. However, I'd bet money if he got a really great cover letter that told him the kinds of things he wanted to know, he'd be influenced by it.

We are all toddlers at heart and like to be told stories

Here's why I think you should write a cover letter even when it's not required and may not even be read. Applying for a job is an exercise in storytelling.

Good stories are always trying to answer a question. Why is Dorothy trying to get to Oz? What made Darth Vader so pissy? How come no one liked Alexander Hamilton?

In your job search you need to ask yourself two important questions: Why them? And Why you? If you can't answer those questions well, it's the wrong organization, the wrong job, or you're not ready for it yet. You will not be successful.

So it helps to work on your storytelling skills.

First, set the scene and make it clear you know what you're headed into. Be clear that you understand what the organization is, what they do, what their values are, and how you could contribute.

By the time you sit down to start writing and adapting your resume for the job, you will have done a ton of research. The first paragraph of the cover letter is where you boil all that down. What do you know about that place and about the person who will be hiring you? Why do you want to work there?

If you're not prepared to answer that question (Why do you want to work here?) you're not ready to apply.

Because I need money! That may be true, but no one cares what you need.

Because I love [whatever the organization does]. Let's say it's books. That may be true, but if you're looking for a job at a library, it's essential to know their mission is as much about providing services to people in need as about spreading the joy of reading. Caitlin Wheeler says, "For a public services associate position we look for somebody who has necessary soft skills. Hard skills we can teach. We need a capacity for empathy and conflict resolution. Customer service experience is directly applicable. Library work is all about providing resources to people as they need them." This is something you would understand if you've read the job description carefully. Library assistants are really doing customer service work, not recommending their favorite mystery novels.

When you do your deep dive to research both the place and the profession, you will have thought about how your values and interests align with their mission. State what you see as their vision (and don't just cut and paste it from their website). Part of your search has to do with identifying these things for yourself.

And then, in the second paragraph, take the opportunity to say how you can aid in that venture. What do you bring? What are your values? What do you care about? Have you overcome a specific obstacle? Did you choose a particularly difficult major like math because you like a challenge, even though you feel you're naturally better at reading literature? Were there projects you wanted to give up on, but you saw them through to completion and got [specific—say them!] results because you are diligent, determined, and dedicated? Committed and hardworking? Passionate and enthusiastic?

Please, however, don't write that you're diligent, determined, and dedicated; committed, hardworking, and detail-oriented; passionate, and enthusiastic.

Those words are meaningless in a resume or a cover letter. Listing them takes up valuable real estate on the only two pages you have (one for a cover letter, one for a resume). I don't know what "dedicated" and "determined" and "hardworking" mean to you. This is where the old creative writing slogan comes into play: *Show, don't tell*. If we can see how you endured a fourteen-degree blizzard helping a doe get her hoof out of a trap, you might be a good candidate for a job as a canine stylist.

A job description will contain keywords you must include in your letter and on your resume. But come on. No one is stupid.* If an employer says they want a passionate and committed person who knows how to use Google Workspace, Teams, Excel, and Tableau, they won't look fondly on someone who writes, "I'm passionate and committed." Guess which keywords they're looking for? Google Workspace, Teams, Excel, and Tableau. And they'd like to know how well you know these programs. That's where certifications can help.

The exercise of writing a cover letter, even if it's not required, will force you to think about how to answer those two most important questions you've asked yourself: *Why them?* and *Why you?* As I'll explain below, if you write in language that sounds like you, you'll have already practiced your responses when you're asked these questions in an interview. Even if the hiring manager never

---

*Well, some people are stupid. They're the ones who repeatedly get the same feedback and keep making the same mistakes.

reads the letter, you'll be better off for having written one. It's part of your preparation, no different from deciding what to wear to an interview.

One of the benefits of writing is it gives us a chance to understand ourselves. The novelist E. M. Forster is often credited with the quote, "How do I know what I think until I see what I say?" Every writer has experienced this. You think you know what the topic is until you start to write and—*Holy zigzag, Batgirl!*—you end up surprised where you got to.

That's why we write shitty first drafts.* We need to get it all down first. I often call the early effort not for public consumption the "vomit version." Then we look at what we've got and clean it up.

Even if you ignore my (excellent!) advice to submit a cover letter, try this: write a terrible first draft to see what you say.

If you end up talking about yourself, your goals, your preferences in a workplace, your desire to start work only after 10:00, or your need to take a yoga class during lunch, please start buying lottery tickets and pray to every deity you can think of to win a cash bonanza. Because the person reading your letter doesn't (yet) care about you or what you want.

Tech company founder Max Mankin is direct about this: "No one is interested in helping you apply your skills or find a rewarding career. That's your job, not ours. In your application, talk about how you can help me/the company, not about how the job helps you 'find yourself.'"

This may sound harsh. I'm pounding on it because I think it's the main mistake people make when applying for jobs. The focus of a cover letter should not be on what you want. And it should not

---

*In Anne Lamott's terrific book on writing (and life), *Bird by Bird*, there's a chapter called "Shitty First Drafts" about the importance of terrible first efforts.

Practical Pro Tip: Making AI Work for You

Bots will be reading what you submit. You may be tempted to use AI to write your cover letter. Depending on how the tech evolves, and how adept you are with prompts, that could be a good way of getting a first draft. Or it could be a whopping mistake.

For each job, you can enter the description, paste in your resume, and ask the AI to do the tailoring for you. That might make drafting easier. However, keep in mind that the bot working for you may also be in the employ of everyone else applying for the same job. And the humans who read cover letters are going to fall asleep reading prose that sounds like a bot. Remember Olivia? She won't be fooled, and she'll have to pour herself more glasses of wine.

When I let AI write a draft for me, the cover letter it came up with made all the mistakes I'm trying to save you from. I sounded like a boring, braggy idiot who cared only about myself and not about how I could contribute. The resulting letter was generic and filled with clichés and was also factually incorrect. (It said I had qualifications it picked up from the job description when I didn't.)

Make sure everything you submit is specific to you and your experience. Even if you use a bot to get started, revise and edit what it produces. You need to sound like the person who will show up for an interview—and hopefully for the job itself.

be about how great you are and how much you've already done. It's meant to answer the only question employers care about: How will hiring you make my life easier?

Mike Bergmann is even more blunt. About most applicants, especially recent college grads, but also PhDs, he says, "They frequently don't realize how little they can contribute right away." Even people who have been trained in various lab procedures will need to be taught how to do things the way his company wants them done.

The best message you can convey is "I want to come and work for you, and I know I don't know anything, but I want to learn and help."

That's the mindset you want to bring to every bit of written material and to the way you present yourself in an interview and the rest of the hiring process.

It's the opposite of the way too many people approach the whole thing.

Here's the simple formula for a good cover letter: Why you, why me, why now.

The salutation

Once you get past the bots, please remember you are a human writing for other humans. That might seem obvious unless, like me, you've read a bunch of letters filled with words no person would ever actually speak aloud in sentences that take effort to plow through. At best they are generic and addressed to some vague "whom" in the ether who will not, I assure you, show much "concern" for what you have to say.

Ditch the "To Whom it May Concern." You might as well say "Greetings, Earthling!"*

My name is not "Hey." Or "Sir." When you have surgery or are injured, the people who work to bring you back to consciousness use your name. Like most mammals and some highly evolved birds, we all respond to our names. No one wants to feel like a cog in a corporate wheel. Plenty of hiring managers say they don't care about such niceties (mostly in tech fields), but you can't go

---

*For certain kinds of geeky tech jobs, that might be funny and appropriate if what follows shows you know something about the company or the person who will be reading your application. There are no hard and fast rules that apply in every situation.

Practical Pro Tip: When You Don't Have a Connection

Often the only name you can find is the recruiter who posted the job on LinkedIn. Address the letter to that person if you must (after looking at a profile). If you don't have a person on the inside who can accept and forward your cover letter and other materials, or an email address for application submission, and there's no place in the formal submission portal for a cover letter, you can try to send the cover letter and resume and other materials to the recruiter through a LinkedIn message.

These people are, for the most part, in the business of collecting application submissions, so they usually do have their LinkedIn profiles set to receive messages from people who are not yet contacts. That extra step will show you are humble, hungry, and smart.

wrong if you remember you're writing to a person and make sure you use their name.

Remember what I said about research? Try to find the name of a person you can address your letter to. You will have then looked them up on LinkedIn and even seen their photo. Here's why this matters: If you remember you are writing to a person and can visualize their face, that will change the way you craft your prose.

Here's what I mean.

When high school students ask me for help with college admissions essays, I often see the same mistakes. The worst essays seem like they were output from computers, using multisyllabic prose that reads as, well, inhuman. But just as bad is when they go too far in the other direction. Instead of remembering an application will be read by a person whose aim is to get to know them, they treat the personal essay as an exercise in creative writing. Bad creative writing.

They might start in medias res—in the middle of a situation—instead of introducing themselves to the reader. They use direct dialogue (one of the hardest things to write well) and sound effects (*Bang! Thwack!*) that work in a comic book but don't do them any favors in an essay. Their prose is full of unnecessary details, and their sentences strain with words they'd never utter aloud.

I read those and think, *Oy.* Then I ask them to write me an email and tell me about themselves. Be as expansive as you can, I say. Think of me as your Auntie Rachel who you rarely see but who's always happy to chat with you at family gatherings.

The emails they send me in response always form the basis for a terrific essay, one that sounds like them, like their real, human selves, since they are written to a specific person, me.

Now, let's be clear. The person reading your cover letter is not your wacky auntie. You don't want to be casual and personal in your approach. Perhaps it's better to think of the recipient as the professor whose classes you loved but who intimidated you so much you could hardly speak in her presence. You always worked hard to impress her. Maybe you came during her office hours and were surprised to see dozens of photographs of the same (photogenic) dog. That made you realize that this person, who seemed so unapproachable, was a doting dog parent.

You'd write to that person with humility and deference, but you'd still want her to like you, and you'd present your best self to them. If you were to email to ask for a letter of recommendation, you might remind them of which class you took with them and when, the concepts from the class that most surprised you, and the readings you most enjoyed. You might mention how much you'd learned in writing that final paper on [here you'd give specifics of what you did in the class]. You could start or end your note with hopes that Harry, the gorgeous mutt whose photo you saw on their desk and heard a bit about, was doing well.

That would be a more effective message than the generic one that says, "I was a student in your ENG 101 course, and I'd like to request a letter of recommendation." It would help your professor do her job—writing you a good, not just positive, recommendation—and acknowledge you're asking for a favor. Not any professor, but me, Rachel, who always has a box of Cheez-Its and a can of diet A&W with a reusable straw on her desk, along with photos of heartthrob Harry.

What, you might wonder, does this have to do with writing a cover letter for a job?

Well, if you think you're writing for a machine, you're likely to come up with something that sounds like computer-generated generic drivel. But if you imagine a real person on the other end, it will create in you a specific mindset. Stephen King, who wrote a great book on writing called, you won't be surprised to know, *On Writing*,* said he thinks every novelist writes for an ideal reader, and his happens to be his wife, Tabitha. He writes to impress her. To make her laugh. To move her. To scare her (in a good way).

What if you can't find a name? That will happen, though if you do a thorough search and network, you're likely to get something. It's okay to write Dear Hiring Manager. Or Dear Recruiter, or Dear Members of the Hiring Committee. Or you can even get more specific. Dear Chocolatiers or Dear Chewy folks.†

And though not everyone is formal, default to formality. If you're sure of someone's pronouns, you can use Mr. or Ms.‡ But I suggest you follow the traditions of writers and simply use their

---

*While I don't love Stephen King's prose, he is a brilliant storyteller and scary smart, and this book is both a terrific read and super useful. I suggest you look at it.
†If writing "dear" sounds formal and old-fashioned, you can use "To the hiring manager."
‡Please don't use Mrs. That is old school for married women only, and at this point in history it should be history.

full name as listed. Dear Stephen King. Even if you feel like you know him, please don't assume you can call him Steve as if you were BFFs. And make sure you don't spell his name as Steven. It's always better to let the other person tell you what they're comfortable having you call them. As I noted in a footnote you may not have read some pages ago, I always tell my students to call me Rachel. Some still default to Professor Toor, and that's fine. But I don't respond to "Hey."

The position you're applying for

Now that you're thinking of the person you're writing to, the next thing is not to create a suspense novel. You are writing to apply for a job. A particular job. It may even have a number attached to it. You need to say right away which one it is, because there may be many openings and many people applying for a variety of positions. Keep this simple and specific.

I am writing to you because I am interested in applying for the position as an entry-level dog stylist at *Woofus* and I am attaching my resume to this message.

Remember: your cover letter should be one page. That's a difficult rhetorical task, because it's far easier to write long than to be concise. One of my favorite quotes is from the philosopher Blaise Pascal: "I would have written you a shorter letter, but I didn't have the time."

This means every paragraph, every sentence, every single freaking word, must earn its keep. You have a lot of ground to cover, and you can't afford sloppiness or flab in your prose. At the end of the book, I've given you a list of tools and tricks to keep things slim and trim. But here's a preview. Let's look at that sentence I just gave you, which may seem perfectly fine.

I am writing to you because I am interested in applying for the position as an entry-level dog stylist at *Woofus* and I am attaching my resume to this message.

Now let's put it on a diet.

Attached is my resume for an entry-level dog stylist position at *Woofus.**

You don't need to say you trust this message finds them well and you hope they're having a good day. Be clear and concise and to the point. I told you to think of the recipient as a person, even though the letter may first be screened by a computer system. Remember whoever comes after that little bot is busy slogging through hundreds of resumes that look pretty much like yours and cover letters addressed to To Whom It May Concern, and they're tired and need to fill this position already. You don't want to waste their time. Remember Olivia.

My advice is to always write long first drafts. Get it all out. Say what you need to say however it comes most naturally to you. Include plenty of vivid and specific details. Then become a ruthless surgeon of your own prose. Learn to take pleasure in getting rid of excess. Whenever you ask someone to read something, you're really asking for their time. Make it pay off or they'll get impatient. You don't have to be an engineer to understand the signal-to-noise ratio. If there's too much junk in the background, the message won't come through.

This is why I tell students taking a course in writing will give them the keys to the kingdom. Writing well is a skill that will serve you in any job and in any situation. Too many people, in-

---

*It would be smart to also include where you saw the job listing. You could add "posted to [Indeed/LinkedIn/your website]."

Practical Pro Tip: Create an Extra Long, Deluxe Version of Your Cover Letter

Write a very, very long draft of the **Why Me** section. Include every single thing you've ever done that might possibly be relevant to some future employment. You can cut and paste and tweak sections of that when you craft individual cover letters. Many of the jobs you'll be applying for will make use of the same experiences and skills, so this long version will be useful. You will want to add to it as you talk to people and discover that you have more to offer than you realized. (We often don't know what makes us special until someone else points it out.)

cluding lots of professors, have said to me, "I'm just not a good writer," as if that's a fact as immutable as having green eyes or topping out at five foot three. Anyone can get better at writing. You want to work on this before the stakes are high—like when you're applying for something you really want. Admission to college, a job, a date.

Why you (the employer)

I've been saying this over and over, yet you still might be tempted to get the order wrong. Imagine you're in a grocery store. Someone is carrying twelve cans of dog food, a bag of kitty litter, and two liters of Diet Coke and is headed toward the exit while you're walking out with a box of Cheez-Its. You both get to the door at the same time. What do you do?

A polite person will open the door and say, "Please, after you." You let the other person go first, right?*

---

*And really, you also open the door for them and maybe even ask if you can give them a hand. Be nice, people!

When you're applying for a job, be polite. Remember: It's not about you. It's about the potential employer. Put them first.

Instead of claiming you're the perfect person for the job (something at this point I know you would never, ever write) and telling them how being hired will help you accomplish your dream of one day styling George Clooney's pig or Amy Tan's Yorkies, you start by showing the research you've done on the organization and saying why it appeals to you. It's the answer to the *Why them?* question you asked yourself earlier.

Make it clear you know who they are and what they do.

If you're applying to work at a law office, you need to know what kind of law they specialize in. At Microsoft or Amazon, which of the eight zillion departments are you applying to? What do they actually do? You can bet the marketing folks are looking for different qualities than the coders.

This is where you can bring in all that networking you've been doing since you started reading this book. It's okay to drop names of people who've told you about the company culture, about new projects that will revolutionize the way people make coffee or find online dates or become rich by investing in carbon capture.

Remember I said the job process depends on storytelling? That doesn't mean you should start with a saga about how you've wanted to be an astronaut since you were a little kid.

Say you want to work for a firm that makes LEDs. You could write about how relieved you were to read that Sylvia Plath also hated physics in high school. But then, in college, a professor showed you that physics explains the world in strange and beautiful ways. You worked harder to conquer math. The ability to apply theoretical concepts to actual problems, like making LEDs brighter and longer-lasting, sounds like more fun than anything you can imagine. You don't yet have the skills or knowledge to do this, but you're eager to learn as much as you can and would be happy to sweep the clean room and wash test tubes.

Anything that shows you are truly interested in the organization and have invested time and energy understanding it helps. Don't say you're resourceful, show it.

Just be judicious. While you might mention something you have in common with the hiring manager, like having attended the same college—as you learned from their LinkedIn profile—don't go into full-on stalker mode and comment on how cute their kids look on Insta or mention the letter to the editor they wrote fifteen years ago. The idea is to personalize while still being professional. Make sure everything is about the job and the organization and how excited you are to be able to contribute.

Why me (the applicant)

All those people who have told you to sell yourself and to proclaim, "I am the most qualified person for this job" at the end of the first paragraph of your cover letter—they are not your friends. They are not doing you any favors. If you're a conspiracy theorist, you might think these are folks who feel competitive with you and want to set you up to fail by giving you bad advice.

Sabrina Mauritz, a community organizer, said the same thing everyone else has said to me, but in an earthy and funny way. When I asked her about mistakes candidates make in cover letters, she told me about this one guy:

> He did that stupid f*cking thing, "Based on the description of this job I believe I am the most qualified person for this job." And I'm just like, who the f*ck are you? It's one thing to say I believe I could be an asset but acting like you are going to save our organization when you are coming in as a beginner stinks to high heaven. If you bring that attitude in, you are going to be unsuccessful in the work. You are going to ruin our relationship.

But here's something to consider. Even though he pissed her off, Sabrina ended up hiring him anyway and told him about his early missteps. She got over her initial reaction because his qualifications were great. She invited him for an interview, and it worked out. Later she told him what a terrible cover letter he'd written.

Ellen Harnick, a lawyer who works at a big nonprofit, was a little more measured when we spoke but she gave the same message: "I really cannot stand the many claims to be 'a perfect fit for your company' or 'the best possible candidate for this role.' Occasionally people who have used this nonsense have turned out to be worth hiring—but we manage to find this out due to concerted efforts." Most employers want to give people the benefit of the doubt and understand they may never have been taught how to present themselves.

As these examples show, it's possible you'll still be hired if you make naive mistakes on your written materials and manage to get to an interview. But hiring managers say nothing is a bigger turn-off than this self-inflating approach—except, perhaps, lying or fudging facts. There's no way for you to evaluate your own perfectness for a job, because so much depends on chemistry. You may have all the skills listed as required, but you may be a person who loves wearing suits and ties and the company is a T-shirt and jeans kind of place. Or vice versa. So even though you may have been told you need to sell yourself, you'll make a better impression if you do show what you've accomplished—and that you're eager to contribute—rather than just assert your perfectness.

How will you be able to contribute? At this point, mostly by showing eagerness to learn and willingness to work your butt off. And this is where you draw on any experiences you've had and translate how the skills you've acquired will be beneficial to them. It's the answer to the *Why you?* question you asked yourself earlier.

Heather Maietta, a professor at Regis College who is an expert in job placement for undergrads, told me a story about her eighth-grade daughter, Emily, who did a school project on building a bridge. She asked Emily what she'd learned. The answer had to do with all the things that go into building a bridge—structural support, arches, construction issues, and so forth.

Yes, but it wasn't just about building a bridge. Professor Maietta helped her daughter think through all the different and transferable skills she acquired along the way: problem solving, teamwork, creativity, open-mindedness, troubleshooting. She would be able to translate that into a story she could tell future employers.

When you start the *Why me* paragraph, try writing a first draft where you tell a story about something you accomplished. Let's say you were able to change the menu in the dining hall to include more vegan options. How did you do this? Well, you got 150 people to sign a petition. Then you emailed a (cranky) demand to the university president, whose assistant thanked you for your input and then, crickets. After a month you respectfully requested a meeting with the vice president in charge of facilities and brought along four other students. You took turns asking questions: How were decisions made about what food is served? How were suppliers selected? Was it possible to have organic produce?

The vice president explained the process, and you wondered whether it might be possible to include more vegan options, since all of you were vegans, as were a lot of others. Many students on your campus didn't want to eat animal products. She said she wasn't aware of that and thought you had a great idea that could easily be accomplished. Later you got a note from the president thanking you for taking the initiative (she clearly had never seen your original, intemperate note).

That's the situation, and here's what you did about it—including a first step that was perhaps not the best move—and the outcome you were able to accomplish. But now do some harder work. It's not what you did in that situation, it's how you can show you will make the employer's job easier. Through this experience, you learned how to work cooperatively with the people in charge and to understand the decision-making process. You came to see how much you didn't know—issues with unions and the burdens small farms face to get food certified as organic. You learned it wasn't as simple as you'd originally thought. But the vice president was appreciative of your attitude and offered you a work-study job in her office.

You might hesitate to include the ill-advised (cranky) demand to the president. But here's what I believe: It's always better to own mistakes than to try to bury them. We learn far more from failure than we do from success. Everyone makes mistakes, but not everyone learns from them. Present yourself as someone open to learning, who can admit when they're wrong without being defensive or making excuses, and who will try to do better in the future. That's the kind of employee and colleague everyone wants to work with.

What if you can't check off all the items on the list of requirements?

Professor Heather Maietta says, "The best thing that a potential employee can write is 'I do not have all the qualifications for this position, but I am eager to learn and will put 100 percent effort into doing that.'"

Professor Maietta advises applying for jobs you are 40 percent qualified for. "That's where the excitement is, and be honest about that." Tell a story that shows how you have all the qualities they are looking for even if not the specific requirements. Let the hiring manager be the one to think, "Oh, she's resourceful, considerate, hardworking, dedicated, determined, passionate, yada yada yada."

How would that look on the page?

Let's say you're applying for a job as a celebrity dog stylist. You know you don't have all the experience listed in the job description. You haven't worked with an A-list celebrity. You have not used different kinds of animal-safe fur dyes. You have not traveled with terrified animals on private planes. You hadn't even heard of some of the breeds mentioned. Until, that is, you googled every one of them, memorized photos, and read enough that you wouldn't mistake a Lagotto Romagnolo for a cockadoodle and that you might expect a Sloughi to need to wear clothes. All you know is you love dogs, and you want to be on photo sets with them.

So what can you say? You might tell a story that shows who you are and the work-appropriate qualities you have to offer. How about the time you saw your elderly neighbor's chihuahua, Brutus, escape from the yard and scoot down the street? Before running after him, you grabbed a piece of ham. Seconds too late, you saw the end of a standoff: a black-and-white striper strutting off, leaving behind a quaking chihuahua. You offered Brutus the ham, scooped up the little stinker, and called your neighbor to tell her that her precious baby would be home soon. You googled what to do next, then slathered Brutus with a mixture of baking soda, hydrogen peroxide, and dish soap. You toweled him off and returned a fluffy, better-smelling good boy to his person.

What does this show about you? Well, you pay attention. You noticed an animal smaller than a cat squeezing under a fence. Instead of sprinting after him, you realized that after a taste of freedom, he might not be so willing to surrender. You thought ahead and brought along a bribe. You knew his person would be worried about him, so once you caught him you called to reassure her. You knew, too, that bathing him would be a chore, especially for an older person. You'd heard that tomato juice was supposed to remove the smell of skunk, but you thought it was best to double-check.* You got the recipe for skunk stank removal, used it, and made sure the little felon was dry.

This story tells me a lot about you. You may not have had any of the experiences required by the job description. But instead of writing that you are resourceful, considerate, and hardworking, you've given a specific example that lets the reader see all of that. Demonstrate, don't articulate. In other words, show, don't tell.

To drive home a point, notice how the stinky dog example says nothing explicit about you, your career goals, or your yen to ride on private jets with your favorite celebrity dog parent. But it does help a reader see how you'll respond to challenges on the job.

When you're doing the *about you* section of the letter, imagine what the job requires—what tasks, what skills, what kinds of problem solving—then make it easy for your future employer to picture you doing it.

Why now

Why now? should be the easiest question for recent grads to answer.

But I want to give you a set of skills to use for the rest of your working life. If you're like most people, you'll change jobs many times during your career. When you want to make a move, you'll always have to explain *why now*. Here's a hint: it can't be your cur-

---

*Your Google search turned up the info that all tomato juice does is give you a red dog, still stinky.

rent job is a dead end, or your boss is a jerk, or the company culture is worse than a Siberian ball-bearing factory. No one wants to hire someone who's disgruntled.

In college you may have had an internship (I hope so) where you were offered a full-time position upon graduation. (How great would that be?)* But you will also have had (I hope) plenty of other experiences—work, academic, and extracurricular— that have given you a taste of what you don't want. This is not the time to mention those.

The answer to *Why now?* must be about looking forward with excitement and enthusiasm and not that you hated making ball bearings or slinging half-caff mocha lattes. Everyone wants a gruntled† employee, not someone who left a previous job in a huff because they felt unappreciated. You don't want to start a new relationship—and remember, all jobs are about relationships—by talking smack about the last one. That is not an attractive look.

So, for a recent grad, while *Why now?* may seem to have an obvious answer, it's another chance for you to underscore once again what you know about the organization, including where it's located. You've spent your entire life in rainy Seattle and now you're eager to move to sunny Southern California. Or, you loved going to college in the Midwest, but you're a New Yorker at heart and would welcome the chance to get back to the land of bialys.

Now, it would be a good idea to start applying for jobs before you're on the street in your robe and mortarboard or have already spent months in your parents' basement playing video games all day. Some jobs need to be filled like, yesterday, so applying while you still have another semester of school may not be a good idea.

---

*This is what happened to me. I'm telling you, it's a fantastic way to start out.
†Gruntled is in the Scrabble dictionary, and I'm sticking with it.

That's when you should be networking, having informational interviews, collecting one or more people who will be willing to mentor you (and even look over your cover letter), and who know in a few months you will hit the market. Ask people about the job cycle. When is a good time to start applying? It will differ by industry, but it's in your interest to learn as much as you can.

The *why now* paragraph is a chance to say you've done the work—graduated from college, explored their company culture, researched what the job requires, are willing to relocate if necessary, and to emphasize how ready you are to try to contribute. It could be as simple as saying, "While I have loved my advanced college chemistry courses, I'm ready to learn to apply my academic work to real-world problems, like the carbon capture plan featured on your website. I can wash test tubes with the best of them and am used to keeping long hours in the lab. I would love the opportunity to learn from your team and eventually be able to contribute."

The sign-off

You don't want to be the person who leaves a party without thanking the host. You need to end your letter with an appropriate and professional sign-off. You have plenty of options here. You can write "Sincerely." Or "Sincerely yours." Or "Best" (I'm a fan of "Best") or "Best regards" or "With respect." Or "Respectfully."* Honestly, this is one of those things that's easy to get right and there's no real advantage in trying to be clever or creative.

Because if it goes wrong, you can give the reader the icks.

I hope I don't have to tell you that "Love" or "XOXO" is not the way to go.

---

*Notice that only the first word is capitalized.

> **Practical Pro Tip: Have Other People
> Read Your Cover Letter to You**
>
> Ask members of your board of directors or your job study group
> to read drafts of your letters aloud to you. Listen to where they
> stumble, or if they autocorrect for you. Then ask what they think.
> If they say there's a problem, believe them and try to figure out
> how you can solve it.

Unless you're British, "Cheers" seems pretentious. (Would you actually say that?) Same goes for "Ciao." Especially if you spell the Italian word as "Chow."

"Thanks" doesn't make sense since they haven't done you any favors. Yet.

"Thanks for your attention" assumes they have, in fact, paid attention. Not clear.

"Warmly," "Fondly," "Affectionately"—presumptuous and icky.

"Looking forward to hearing from you." Begging the question.

"Take care," "Have a nice day," "Be well"—who are you to give commands?

You want to call attention to the things that matter; that's all the stuff between the salutation and the sign-off.*

Three, two, one—contact!

If the letter does its job, the hiring manager will want to get in touch with you. Make it easy. No one will go on a Google hunt

---

*By now you know me well enough to know I wanted to end this section with "XO, Rachel."

to get your phone number. And yes, realize it's possible many people, especially those who have been old enough to drink for a while, will (*gasp!*) call you on the phone.

Now, even though I've been getting into bars legally for a very long time, I've managed to catch the young person's disease of avoiding calls except with my closest friends. I don't let my phone put through numbers not on my contact list. But if I've sent a bunch of emails or LinkedIn messages (not texts! never texts!) to people I'd like to ask for the favor of their time, I switch the setting so unknown numbers come through and folks can reach me.

If I don't answer immediately, I check that my voicemail isn't full and I listen to all messages. Recruiter Mikki Hubbard says, "The phone is your friend." She gets frustrated when applicants don't listen to their voicemail. She says, "Make sure your phone number is under your signature in every email communication. Don't make me look for it."

You should also put your contact information on every page of your cover letter and resume. Because I live in Washington State and often talk to people in New York and Chicago, I need to be aware of time zone differences when I make appointments. I'm embarrassed to say I sometimes screw them up when scheduling Zoom calls with college buddies. And not just with them. Recently I had been in touch with a book editor in New York. I was so eager to chat I took the first time slot she said she had available: 9:30 a.m.

Fortunately, the night before the call I realized that meant 6:30 a.m. my time, not half past noon. The gracious editor laughed it off. But if it had been an interview for a job I wanted, one that required attention to detail, and I was logging on at noon just to be ready, well, you can guess how that might have gone.

So, list your email and your phone number, and you also might want to say what time zone you're in, especially if you don't want

Practical Pro Tip: A Cover Letter Checklist

Make sure your cover letter shows you are

- Writing to a specific person
- Interested in this particular organization—and why
- Applying for a specific position
- Able to show relevant experience
- Attaching what you've said you'll attach (your resume)
- Contactable (phone number, email, and time zone)

to get a call at 6:00 a.m. You don't have to put your street address, but you can include city and state.

Quick Takes

- The simple formula: Why you, why me, why now.
- Make a case for yourself even if you may not seem an obvious choice.
- Make the person reading the letter feel valued, and make them see you understand what they do.
- Even if it's not required, send a cover letter.
- Applying for a job is an exercise in storytelling.
- Put your contact information on every page: include email, phone, and even your physical location on your materials. And make sure you say what time zone you're in. At this point, area codes tell us zip.
- Ditch the "To Whom It May Concern"—try to find a name.
- Default to formality.
- The cover letter should be one page.
- People are busy—don't waste their time.

- It's not what you did, it's what you're going to be able to do: "I do not have all the qualifications for this position, but I am eager to learn and will put one hundred percent effort into doing that."
- Employers want to know what you truly care about.
- Make sure you can receive phone calls, and check your voicemail.

6 *The Resume*

The Danish philosopher Søren Kierkegaard said life can only be understood backward, but it must be lived forward. This is also true of resumes. You might not even realize how your past experience has prepared you for your next steps. Writing a resume is a chance to reflect.

And for many jobs, the resume is the document that matters most.

With one page to get past the bots, you must show *how* and *why* you are the right person for *this* job so you will be invited to meet a human. That's a high-stakes assignment.

Many people become more concerned with how their resume looks than with the content. This is a mistake. If it's too fancy, with graphics or lines of type crawling up the sides, the little trash-can robot will give up trying to read it, and into the bin it will go.

The same is true for the humans. Anytime you make it hard for someone to get the information they need, it's easier for them to file that document in the garbage.

It's simple to find an online template, and there's no reason not to use one. In the old days, when people printed resumes, those who put theirs on pink scented paper stood out. And not in a good way. And here's an easy tip: leave it as a Word document

**Practical Pro Tip: Create an Extra Long,
Deluxe Version of Your Resume**

This may be two pages or twenty. Include any possibly relevant information and language you might use to describe what you did and what skills you gained from each experience. Use short, simple bullet points and include **quantifiable** results. This deluxe version is one you will never submit.

Copy this version and delete everything not relevant to the specific job. Then change the language to match **exact** words used in the job description. Don't forget to add bullet points with the revised language to your deluxe resume for future use. You now have a way to customize your resume that will prove more useful over time. And fifteen minutes may be all it takes to do this for each job.

instead of putting it into PDF form. That way the system will be able to read it and spit it back out in a way that makes sense. Don't rely on formatting to make yourself stand out.

The main thing to remember is each resume must be customized, and though it won't take a lot of time, if you don't take that step you might end up in the bin. If you're applying to ten different jobs, you need ten different resumes.

You'll want to include your education (degree, institution, possibly dates). For some fields, like hard sciences, maybe include your GPA and relevant coursework, as well as your job or volunteer experience, skills, and maybe hobbies. I'll explain each of these below, but remember that while every industry wants to see different information, everything on your resume must work together to tell a story. What's the moral of that story? By this point you should know: *Here's how my experience will make your job easier.*

You've got one page to make a case for yourself.

Some people include an objective, purpose, or summary statement at the top. The risk is this takes up valuable space. It can be useful if a cover letter isn't required or in a field where people (say they) don't read them.

Remember, though, I advised you to include a cover letter anyway. The worst case is it won't be read. But you will have gone through the important exercise of writing the reasons you want to be hired at this particular organization.

If your summary statement goes something like, "Hardworking, compassionate, detail-oriented, and energetic college graduate," you might as well skip it. These are all traits you need to show based on your experiences. Omit meaningless words.*

Cheryl Chamberlain says McKinstry likes to see a statement of purpose that shows dedication: "I have devoted my education to learning more about climate change." This is powerful, and she will look for ways you've done that, maybe by writing a senior thesis on disappearing glaciers or by volunteering at a recycling plant.

For librarian Caitlin Wheeler, an objectives statement is a chance to list your aspirational goals—for example, to promote social justice by helping provide access for underserved communities.

Recruiter Robin Schachter advises, "Use LinkedIn to offer a few sentences about your objective/interests/goals in a less formal manner than the resume."†

---

*You will find this advice in Strunk and White's little book *The Elements of Style*, which may be lingering somewhere on your parents' bookshelf. And in the last chapter, I'll give you some tips.

†Robin has so much advice about LinkedIn she helped me create the Pro Tip on using it, even though my dog Harry peed on her kitchen wall when he was a puppy.

Getting past the bots

Customize your resume by picking up language from the job description, and include all the important keywords. If a library job includes "customer service" and you've been a barista, bingo! You have "customer service" experience. But if on your resume you write "customer care," you won't match. If it calls for someone who knows Microsoft Excel, list that under your skills. Make sure you incorporate the organization's language. Phrase everything *exactly* the way it appears in the ad, and pay close attention to details. If something in the job description is abbreviated, use that abbreviation and no other.

Numbers are your friends

No one wants to see vague generalities on a resume. Hiring managers like metrics. Numbers. Quantities. This is something many people fail to consider when thinking about their experiences.

Recruiter Wenda Cenexant says, "Almost everything you do you can quantify." You can say "I worked with X number of people daily." Or "There were X number of pages in the books I had to create." As a member of a college club, how many new members did you recruit? You worked as a cashier at Target—for how many hours a week?

Sabrina Mauritz says, "Numbers are good because they show scale and depth of commitment. If someone says, 'I got 5,000 petition signatures,' tell me how you got them. 'I helped organize a protest and there were ten people.' Actually, a ten-person protest can be more effective than a hundred-person protest. I want to know what your role was. I want to hear results!"

Work experience: Say what you did, clearly

Most people would describe themselves as "hardworking" if they want to get a job. But this is your chance to show what that looks like in your life. If you didn't take part in extracurricular activities on campus because you couldn't afford to live in a dorm and had to drive forty-five minutes each way to get to class, then had to pick up your little brother after school five days a week, you might not think to explain that. Taking family responsibilities seriously shows character.

But if it looks like you did nothing other than go to class, you never had an internship or work-study job, and your summers are unaccounted for, you need to explain how you spent your time. If it was reading nineteenth-century Russian novels—and you're applying for a job in publishing—you might say that. How many pages of Dostoyevsky and Tolstoy did you get through each week in addition to the long list of books required in your English major? (Just don't expect anyone to hire you because your resume is in a font that mimics Cyrillic.)

Recently I saw a resume that listed time volunteering in a community kitchen with this description: "Ensured the cleanliness of dinnerware and utensils." Yikes! If you were a dishwasher, just say so. There's no shame in cleaning up. Even better if you can add you worked X hours a week in a kitchen that served X number of meals to X number of people.

Remember, most of us have pretty good BS detectors. Sabrina Mauritz brings this home. She says, "If you're describing efforts or projects that you were involved with and can't speak to your own role, I don't believe you had a real role. It's important to actually be able to say the tasks you did and the skills you've used."

She gives an example: "If you say, 'I was part of this multiracial coalition that used this process for conflict management and this process for consensus decision making,'" she'll ask herself, "What was your role and what were the results? Are you showing up at the meetings and being a really nice white person who's nodding when Black people talk, or are you putting yourself in a position to cultivate an environment of inclusivity?"

Recruiter Mikki Hubbard says, "Show me that you picked up something [in college, in summer jobs, in volunteer opportunities] about the working world. Was there a special project you did—maybe created a poll, did a task (it doesn't have to be a huge task) but something that will show me what you've learned, that it isn't your first time in a corporate environment?"

She continues, "I don't care about high school unless you were valedictorian or class president. What you did in college will count, particularly if it was an activity that forces you to put yourself out there, like being a member of debate team all four years. That shows me you can think on your feet. If you DJed a show on college radio or played a sport, you have demonstrated that you can manage multiple priorities—that might potentially be transferable to a sales job."

Start-up founder Max Mankin says, "Don't include your experience lifeguarding and being a cashier for technical jobs—unless they are directly relevant to the job you are applying for." And, remember, they might be. Perhaps under a bullet point about lifeguarding you mentioned you learned to respond to emergencies. You are certified in CPR and are calm under pressure. It's your mission to think about how to translate these experiences. Just listing them won't be enough, but it's possible you can put them to use as plot points in the story your resume is telling. Increasing responsibility. Quick reactions. Attention to detail.

Mankin also says, "Academic projects and classes aren't unique enough to set you apart. Show some relevant intern work or research lab experience. Start early on this in your high school or college career."

He's right. *Unless* you undertook an academic project that shows your commitment to the problems his company is trying to solve. If you did an independent study because you wanted to learn how to code, that could be relevant if the job you're applying for involves programming. The effectiveness of how and what you list depends on the attitude that comes through. Hiring managers want to see applicants who are curious and work hard to learn what they don't know.

Don't lie, don't exaggerate

Anything you put on your resume (and cover letter and LinkedIn and possibly even social media) will be fair game for interview questions. If you describe your capstone project, be prepared to explain whether you worked alone or were a member of a team. Even though it may seem like a national pastime to lie and cheat, in this age of fact-checking by our good friend Google, please, I beg you, be honest.

When you do a job search, you write a resume. Maybe you stay at the same job for several years and then, when you're ready to make a move, you use that first version and build on it. That makes perfect sense. The problem is if you include something that's not true you risk perpetuating a big fat lie.

Here's a weird cautionary tale.

In 2007 the dean of admissions at MIT, Marilee Jones, lost her job for lying on her resume. While she claimed she had degrees from three universities—Albany Medical College, Union College, and Rensselaer Polytechnic Institute—in fact the dean of admissions at MIT, who had denied admission to scads of brilliant applicants, had never even attended attended any of those schools.

In an interview with NPR, Jones said, "I just slid that under the door, and honestly, I forgot all about it." I find that hard to believe, especially given that in her job she saw how students often inflated their own accomplishments.

She had even been using the honorific "Dr." Finally someone called her out. After nearly three decades in college admissions, she had to come clean. She resigned in disgrace. Now she runs a college consulting business where she advises applicants. She ended her NPR interview with this: "I think the whole system is almost set up for kids to lie." And maybe adults too. Please, do not lie. Don't even exaggerate. It's far more effective and compelling just to say, "I haven't done that yet but I'm eager to learn."

No one expects you to be perfect. Failure is fine—what matters is what you've learned and how you describe it. At his semiconductor company, Mike Bergmann liked to see GPAs on resumes. A low one could be a red flag. *Unless* there's an explanation. If your schoolwork suffered because you were hospitalized or worked three jobs or had some issue that you can explain, show that on your resume, and especially in your cover letter.

Gaps

At this point, if you're a recent grad, you won't have to worry much about time unaccounted for in your work history. It's perfectly acceptable—advisable, even—for high school students to take a gap year before starting college. And it's OK to take some time off during school—maybe to travel, or to work to make money to pay for college, or because lots of people get stressed out and need to stay home for the sake of their mental health. Or, say, there's been a pandemic that made education on Zoom neither fun nor effective.

You will have had a few summers when you weren't in school. If you didn't work or get an internship or volunteer walking your neighbor's pig, think of a way to describe how you spent your time.

A good bullet point will be truthful and directly relevant to the job. If you're looking for work in publishing, you might explain that you spent the summer reading works by Black and Latinx queer women. If you want to work at a tech start-up, it makes sense that you used your summer to develop an app to track dogs gone AWOL. Or you hiked all the fourteeners in Colorado, which helped you decide to apply for a job as a park ranger.

As with everything, translate what you did into something—a skill, an interest, a mindset—that will be of use and interest to the person who is in a position to hire you for a specific job. You can put this on your resume under "summer experiences" or "hobbies." There's no one right answer.

Don't be embarrassed about your work experience

If you're applying for a job at a fancy-pants investment bank and you haven't been able to do an unpaid internship because in the summer you have to work on your family's farm or get a job in a factory, include that on your resume. Bucking sixty-pound bales of hay in triple-digit heat to store enough feed for two dozen horses and then teaching yourself calculus in the evenings is a lot harder than shadowing bankers. You can show your resilience and grit and work ethic and all the things employers want even if it seems as if the work wasn't directly relevant. It's up to you to make the case that the ability to work independently and sweat it out will translate to what they need. ("Worked on family farm.

Bucked sixty-pound bales of hay, moved irrigation pipe in three ten-acre fields, and mucked twenty-four stalls a day.")

Hobbies: Tell me what you pay attention to and I'll tell you who you are

If you haven't gotten the message by now, just as there's no universal answer to the question What is the meaning of life?* each job application will vary depending on the industry, the organization, the hiring manager, and, well, you.

I'm reluctant to say exactly what to include when it comes to hobbies because there's so much individual variation in how the information will be received. Some employers care only about your work history, and others love to see how you spend your free time. Use your network to ask if listing hobbies is a good idea. When you're starting out in the working world, you may not have a lot of other information to convey, so describing your interests can be a way to show who you are and what you care about.

"I want employees who are sad, tired, and disillusioned," joked Matt Furst, marketing manager at a tech firm that hires lots of creative writing graduates. He explained that the jobs he has to fill pay well, but they're not anyone's dream. He wants to know potential employees have interests outside work that will fulfill them and bring them joy and that they've given up on finding self-actualization on the job.

Even though she does offer a dream job for someone who loves to read—as assistant to the editorial director of Farrar, Straus and Giroux Books for Younger Readers—Joy Peskin feels it is important those who work for her have plenty of interests and passions. She says, "What do you love doing *outside* of work? I'm looking

---

*Some older folks might argue the answer is 42.

for people who have a life outside of their career. I don't care what you do in the evenings or on the weekends—singing or dancing or crafting or playing Dungeons and Dragons or volunteering, whatever—but if you work for me, we are not working all the time. We have to live life so we can edit books about life."

In science, finance, and tech fields, hiring managers may feel different. On resumes, Mike Bergmann doesn't want to see any hobbies not directly related to the job he's trying to fill. "I'm looking for action. If someone says they are 'passionate' about something, I want to see that they did something to achieve a goal in that area. The particular area of interest isn't key, but rather the energy and determination that went into achieving the goal are the metrics of value." Building a Tesla coil in your backyard? Making a go-cart from junk you've collected? That will intrigue him, and he'll want to hear about it.

It's important to understand what our hobbies say about us.

Years ago I heard a memorable story from a friend who clerked for the late Supreme Court justice Byron White. In college, White had been a runner-up for the Heisman Trophy and took a leave of absence from Yale Law School, where he'd earned the highest grades in his class, to play in the NFL. He led the league in rushing as a rookie.

Until the tail end of his career, White refused to discuss his football years. When people would see him and say, "Hey, you're Whizzer White," he'd answer, "I used to be." The Supreme Court justice didn't want people to see him as just a football player. That probably had something to do with his own insecurity. When you're applying for a job, make sure you're showing the parts of yourself you're proud of and that will translate into what employers like to see.

Being excellent at something that requires both talent and discipline often translates to other areas in life. Many hiring managers say they like to see applications from athletes. They can expect a good work ethic and an ability to get along with others. Team membership can lend a shared sense of identity. We all like people who have interests that align with ours. When I meet someone who runs ultramarathons, or rides horses, or has had a pet rat or a Vietnamese pot-bellied pig as a companion, or who can't wait for the latest Louise Penny novel, I'm excited to talk to them.

But I'm just as eager to learn about things I know little about. If you say you fold origami, or bake elaborate pastries, or worked in a funeral home, or went to a high school with a graduating class of fourteen, that's all information that you can put in bullet points on your resume and people will find it interesting.

How we spend our free time shows much about who we are. It's important to consider the message you send when you list your activities, interests, and hobbies. Scuba diving, ski racing, and flying airplanes come with hefty price tags. If you do those things I might assume your parents have plenty of money. It's fine to be privileged (frankly, I'm jealous), but it's never okay to have an attitude of entitlement. How you explain these hobbies will show an employer who you are.

If you're a nationally ranked equestrian and explain that to help pay for your horse you spend thirty hours a week at the barn mucking stalls and giving lessons to little kids, that reads differently than if you list a bunch of awards. If your ski racing is funded by a summer job working at a warehouse and waiting tables on the weekends, it looks a lot different from sponging off your parents. If you're fortunate to have a family that provides you with opportunities others might not be able to afford, that's wonderful. How can you show that you're willing to work hard and contribute?

You will have to decide, for each job, which hobbies and interests are directly relevant. If you're applying to work as a veterinary technician, experience with horses is perfect. If you want to work in a lab that requires attention to detail, explain that ski racing requires a complicated understanding of which waxes are appropriate for changing conditions and that it can take hours to get different pairs of skis ready.

Some busy employers will look at someone's resume for the first time when they're sitting across the desk from them. They'll scan the hobbies and ask about those first, if only to give themselves a chance to read the employment and experience sections.

As with everything you put on the page—and I'll say this over and over and over—good writing is vivid and specific. (Also concise: remember, you've got one page.) If you're tempted to put "traveling" as a hobby, that tells me less than if you say you took a solo trip to Thailand, Cambodia, and Laos. Or you borrowed a van and road tripped with three friends to seven national parks in the western United States.

Frankly, I would no more list reading as a hobby, interest, or activity than I would eating, brushing my teeth, or breathing. For me it's an essential part of life. When I go into someone's home, I scan their bookshelves. There I learn much about who they are and what they care about. If you love to read, list your favorite authors. If you're applying for a job at a tech company, you might include science fiction books, which would be expected, or recent memoirs by authors of color or translations of novels from India and Africa, which may not be.

Think about the person who will read your resume and the questions you now know she will ask herself: *How will hiring you make my job easier? And will you be a good match for this organization?* If she's worried that you grew up sheltered and isn't sure how you'll fit into a global and diverse culture, a broad reading list can show you have interests beyond your direct experience.

**Practical Pro Tip: Do Not Type Answers
Directly into Little Boxes Online**

Many applications will give you a little box where you can write 100 to 200 words (they'll give a limit) about why you want the job or what qualifications you have. **Stop right there.** Do not just start typing. Read the question and then open a Word document (or take out a notepad). Take the time to craft these answers. Even if the question seems simple, like "How did you hear about this job," spend time on the response. All of this will be uploaded into your file in an applicant tracking system. The hiring manager can hit different tabs to see your transcript, your resume, your experience, and the answers to these questions. It's all official, and it all matters. In the words of Ellyn Foltz's father, sometimes you have to slow down to speed up. Take the time to do this right. It may seem easy to just type words into these little boxes. Don't do it. (Yes it's easy, but easy isn't always right.)

What not to include

Remember: include only things directly relevant to each specific job and organization. It's great if you were the captain of the swim team in your high school.* But that was a while ago, and it matters a whole lot less than if you graduated from college summa cum laude.

That spelling bee from eighth grade? No. Delivering newspapers or babysitting in high school? No.

There are countries where it is customary to have a photo on the resume. For jobs in the United States, you'll look like a weirdo

---

*Some schools have fourteen captains of the swim team. Let's leave all this padding behind, shall we?

if you include one. You should, however, have a professional-looking headshot on your LinkedIn page.

Employers are not allowed to ask about marital status, sexual orientation, race, disability, or any other protected categories. If it's relevant to the job—say you are applying to work for an organization that supports undocumented farmworkers—you might want to include the fact that you speak Spanish. You don't need to give your ethnicity, though talking about your background is fair game in the interview, especially if you relate it to why you want the job.

We all use acronyms and jargon to make things easier for ourselves. But don't assume everyone will know what ASEWU stands for. If they see you've gone to Eastern Washington University, they may figure out it's Associated Students of Eastern Washington University, but it could also mean something else. Spell out anything not obvious to someone who is outside your small world. We all live in small worlds.

Keep the language professional. If your title during a summer job was "evangelist," you might want to include in parentheses that you did social media for a start-up tech company. And if the company name was F&#@, you will likely want to give a brief description of what they did. The more things make someone stop and wonder, the less likely they are to want to talk to you.

How to put it together

I told you this book won't give you specific recipes. Instead, I want to help you think about how to approach the various parts of getting a job.

A ton of free stuff is available online—templates for layouts, long lists of action verbs, examples of resumes. As with all things, you get what you pay for. I'd stick to sites that are connected to

Practical Pro Tip: Keeping Track of Resume Versions

Since you will tailor your resume for each job, make sure you keep track of which version you have submitted and review it before the interview. This is critical so that you don't look flustered if someone starts asking you questions from your resume during the interview. Also, bring a paper copy or be prepared to email a copy of that exact resume during the interview. If hiring managers can't find your resume in their own system, you'll look polished if you can say, "Hold on, I'll send it right to you." You may want to save copies on your phone as well as your computer.

real organizations, like colleges, or companies like LinkedIn. A lot of enterprising and entrepreneurial youngsters with zero relevant experience have created TikToks to, um, help you. You'll have to be judicious in whose advice you heed.

In this case it's best to do a lot of research. (Big surprise, right?) Pay attention when you're hearing the same things over and over. If there's something you haven't seen anywhere else, including anything you've read in this book, go to someone in the network of mentors you've created and ask their opinion. Is it appropriate to include your personal pronouns on a resume? People in some industries will say yes, absolutely, and others may look at you like you have two heads. There are, believe it or not, plenty of people who don't understand why someone may not automatically use the pronouns that seem to go with the gender of their name.

Each industry requires different things. As you search for jobs, you may find that while you thought you wanted to work in investment banking, insurance feels like a better match. Or perhaps you want to stay put and work for the university you just graduated from. A job in student affairs requires a different resume than a job in the registrar's office.

As with everything you ever put on a page (electronic or otherwise), you don't want the first person (or robot) to read it to be the one in a position to reject you. Get other people to look over everything before you click Submit. And, please, read everything you write *out loud*. Or get Microsoft Word to do it for you as you read along and make corrections. You will have many corrections to make.

Quick Takes

- Resumes must be customized for each job.
- One page is enough—and think of that as valuable real estate.
- Everything has to work together to tell a story.
- Pick up language from the job description and include all important keywords.
- Hiring managers need to see metrics, numbers, quantities.
- Nothing beats honesty.
- Anything on the resume is fair game for interview questions.
- Remember Mr. Rogers: what's mentionable is manageable.
- A good answer will be truthful and directly relevant to the job.
- Your hobbies say a lot about you.

7 The Interview

After reading your cover letter, a hiring manager liked the way you described your enthusiasm for the mission of their organization, and from your resume sees that you've worked hard to teach yourself Spanish and Chinese. Now they want to meet you. Yikes!

Each organization will have a different procedure

Often an initial interview is the first step in a process that can take months. You may start with a series of video responses that you record in the comfort of your bedroom, move on to a half-hour phone call, then be invited to meet with a human resources person or a lower-level employee, and then have a team interview. For some jobs you might be taken to lunch or dinner.

A lot of organizations will ask you to perform specific tasks. You might need to use a whiteboard to do sample calculations or make a sketch. You might have to take a proofreading test or create a writing sample. You could be asked to do a short presentation about your senior thesis. You'll be evaluated on how you answer questions and your ability to communicate. You may even be asked to do what seems like real work on a real project—before you're even hired.

Take all these tasks seriously. You can ask in the initial interview what the hiring sequence is typically like so you have some idea of what to expect (if they don't spell it out for you), and you can ask people in your network what they went through when they were hired.

What is totally within your control is your attitude, and that will make a big difference in how people respond to you. Are you curious and enthusiastic and ready to contribute?

Employers are looking to fill their positions. They want to hire you. Make it easy for them.

A quick phone call is your first opportunity not to blow it

While it's likely that you will get an email asking you to schedule a short phone interview, plenty of busy hiring managers, especially older ones, will start the interviewing with a phone call. To repeat: make sure your phone is set to receive unknown numbers. And answer when it rings. Make sure your outgoing message is professional and, please, check your voicemail. And your email. Frequently. Do you really want to miss a job interview because you forgot to check messages? Or because you neglected to clear them? It is frustrating for someone who wants to hire you to be unable to leave a message.

When the phone rings, you'll be asked if you know what the job is and why you're interested. If you can't answer those questions, briefly and without a lot of BS, you need to do more research. Before they call.

As I've said, the main thing employers look for—also your main thing—is a match. Are you someone they'll be comfortable working with? Can you learn and grow and succeed, and will hiring you make their job easier?

Practical Pro Tip: Phone Interviews

Maintain your calendar so you can respond immediately to a request to schedule an interview. Propose a few time blocks when you can be in a quiet place with good reception.

If someone calls to do a screening interview, you can say, "I'm excited to speak with you. Can I get your number and call you back in ten (or twenty or thirty) minutes so I can move to a quiet place away from distractions? This conversation is important, and I want to be able to give you the information you need." No one with integrity will refuse this request. If they do, you've just learned something about what it would be like to work there.

When you're talking on the phone, realize your interviewer is likely at a computer with questions on the screen. They will type each of your answers into little boxes. Make it easy on them. Answer simple yes or no questions with yes or no. If you have more you want to share, first answer yes or no and then ask if they'd like you to expand. Don't ramble on. It's hard to get the balance right (I know, you're nervous), but eventually the interviewer will get to more open-ended questions that will allow you to answer at greater length.

To remember that you're talking to a person, find them on LinkedIn or on the company's website and look at their photo while you're on the phone. Also, it can help to have on hand the job description and the version of your resume you submitted.

If you're nervous, you're normal

We all get nervous, especially regarding things we care about. Plenty of big-name entertainers suffer from paralyzing stage fright. People at the top of their careers can still get the shakes when they have to perform or give a talk. I sure do.

If you're nervous in an interview, you're human. It's normal. You can even say, "I'm nervous." In fact, you buy yourself some

Practical Pro Tip: Make Notes for Each Job

Make notes and have them with you. Include the top three reasons you want the job at that particular organization and the most
important things you want to convey about your experience. List
what you know about the company. Have a list of good specific
questions. You can use these notes in video and phone interviews and in person. Bringing notes to the interview makes you
look prepared and serious. But make sure you pay attention to the
conversation and don't just read off your cheat sheet.

empathy because we've all been there, and interviewers, if they're
good, will understand and try to help you relax. It's easy to spin
out, to find yourself in a bind and keep talking and talking and
talking. That's not great. It's also not great to withdraw to the
point that you come off as aloof and uninterested.

So practice saying, "Can I have a minute to regroup?" It's okay
to take a breath. If you care about getting the job, the stakes feel
high. Showing you care—even if it's your body's autonomic nervous system making you sweat—is actually endearing. No one
will fault you. What matters is how you handle yourself. Honesty
and authenticity go a long way.

Recorded or video interviews are still interviews

Since many organizations now do initial screenings on video calls
or plain old phone calls, they may not be able to see you sweat. In
fact you may feel more comfortable because you're at home.

Lots of us are now used to Zoom and other video chats. During
the pandemic, it was a weird and intimate way of getting to know
people. We met a lot of cats. We saw the art on people's walls, light
sabers on the floor, and parents hovering in the background and

chiming in. That was fine in the context of education. When it comes to job interviews, think about how you present yourself. The key to interviews—and, really, to the whole job search—is to be the best version of yourself for that job. And also, to realize you don't have to bring your whole self to work.

What do I mean by that? Code-switching. Many of us don't behave or speak in the same way when we're with our friends as when we're talking to professors. Parts of our personality that come out with family members, we learn to keep hidden from strangers. You want to be happy in a job, and that means finding a good match. And showing up as the most professional version of yourself.

Some big organizations use third parties to do initial online interviews. Phil Gardner, director of the Collegiate Employment Research Institute at Michigan State University, explains the process, "Students log in, video captures them, questions scroll at the bottom," and they respond.

Easy, right?

Except, he says, they sometimes "show up in pajamas, drinking beer, and neglect to think about how serious it is."

Be aware of your background, your clothes (at least from the waist up), whether you're muted, or if there's a cat in heat screeching in the yard. Or in your room.

Also know that some AI software allows the bots to analyze things like facial expressions or linguistic patterns. There are all sorts of ways to be screened out; you just need to focus on doing the best job you can and being authentic in your eagerness and humility.

This is even more important when you're doing a live video interview.

Mikki Hubbard says you need to show poise. Maybe have the camera face a plain white wall, not the Metallica poster. Hubbard

Practical Pro Tip: Zoom Interviews

If you can, stand while doing a video interview. This allows for better posture, breathing, and composure. Position your phone or computer high enough (on a stack of books or a shelf or whatever it takes) that you can look straight ahead. Practice smiling when talking, even on the phone. Interviewers can "hear" the smile.

Use Post-it notes to identify the three to five bullet points you have decided you must get across during the call. Swap them out as you prepare for each call.

says, "Avoid backlighting, which creates shadowing on your face, and turn off ceiling fans, which can produce a strobe effect." If there's a lot going on in your room, use the function to blur your background. You want the focus to be on you, not the purloined "Men at Work" road sign hanging over your bed.

Practice. I had a meeting scheduled with someone, and just before it started I noticed the invitation was for Microsoft Teams. I had never used Teams, even though it's common in corporate settings. I scrambled to download it, and once it opened I couldn't, um, touch up my appearance the way I could on Zoom. I wished I'd brushed my hair and spackled on some makeup.

Whatever platform you'll be interviewing on, make sure you're comfortable with it. Make sure the lighting is good and that your head isn't cut off. As Mikki Hubbard says, "You don't want the venue of the interview to be the reason you don't get the job."

Project Runway

I won't spend much time on clothing. But, like proofreading your cover letter or resume, using the correct (and correctly spelled) name of the organization, and not doing a recorded video interview with unbrushed hair and in pajamas, you need to figure out how to dress for each interview.

You don't have to buy a new wardrobe. Your college career center may have a "closet" you can borrow interview clothes from. You don't want to be uncomfortable, just put together. It helps to know something about the company culture (network!), but even if it's a T-shirt and jeans kind of place, like the start-up founded by millennial Max Mankin, he says, "Be formal. Overdress." (Also, he says, "Show up on time. Take notes.")*

You should look like yourself, but the professional version who will come to work on time and ready to contribute. Dress to be respectful and not disruptive. If you're unsure whether something is appropriate, ask for help. And don't ask a friend. Ask someone who works in an environment like the one where you'll be interviewing.

Yes, they are judging you

You will be evaluated from the first contact until you start work (and after). And not just in the interview. If you're nice to the people in power but haughty and dismissive with assistants, that will bite you on the butt.

Mike Bergmann likes to walk people to their cars and peeks in the windows. If he's hiring someone to work in a "clean room" in a lab that requires donning paper bunny suits, he doesn't want to see Doritos bags and empty Mountain Dew cans on your passenger seat.

On the other hand, Matt Furst, who looks for quirky, techy

---

*Introverts can become too focused on their note taking and fail at interviewing because they are not connecting to the people in the room (either in person or virtually). So don't spend all your time taking notes—be judicious and remember it's not a class, it's a discussion.

people to do marketing work, loves seeing into the lives of those he wants to hire. He'll want to know about those candy bars you love so much. Matt wants people who have lives outside work, while Mike doesn't care. Again, this has to do with company culture, hiring manager, and industry. You are looking for the right match—and so are they.

Recently I heard a story about a hiring manager from a construction company who met a bunch of students at a job fair and at the end invited those who remained out for drinks.

They drank. He paid. They drank more. He kept paying.

And then he set up interviews for early the next morning.

The career center director who told me the anecdote explained, "Part of the job is to entertain clients. Successful candidates were those who had one drink or none and showed up the next morning sharp and ready to engage."

You may feel comfortable in an interview and make a good connection with the hiring manager and with other people at the organization. This is what you want. But remember you are being evaluated every step of the way. These folks are not your friends, though it would be great if they become pals after you've been in the job for a while. However, it's a mistake to get too familiar before you're hired.

If you're someone who gets excited and wants to add to ideas, make sure you are listening. Attorney Jay Manning says it's not good when someone is "talking more than they listen, if they're so eager to get their words out they run over the last part of the question."

Or worse, interrupting. Matt Furst says, "In interviews, I can be a slow talker. I notice when someone interrupts or talks over me, and it's a little irritating. But it really bothers me when they interrupt someone on my team."

Remember, your job is to blend into their organization and prioritize their goals. Show how you will contribute to a team.

Jennifer Cast was an early employee of a little start-up in Seattle you may have heard of. She told a story about hiring someone. She offered him the job at Amazon, but he was also considering an offer from another company. Over a period of weeks, he kept waffling and discussing both jobs with her, acting as if she were a confidante. Eventually she told him he didn't seem excited about working for her and he should go ahead and take the other job. She withdrew the offer.

What questions to expect

In a quick online search you can find lists of hundreds of interview questions. Some will be specific to industries. Some will be wackadoodle. If you get a bad interviewer, or someone who wants to see how you perform under pressure, you might get asked something you could never have anticipated ("Was 9/11 an inside job?" "If you were a vegetable, which one would you be?")

If you apply for work that requires logic and problem solving, you might be asked a "Fermi question." This requires you to come up with a rough estimate of something you couldn't possibly know an exact answer to. It's named after physicist Enrico Fermi, who estimated the strength of the atomic bomb at the Trinity test site by throwing scraps of paper into the air to see how far they traveled after the denotation. The point: to reckon the order of magnitude. If you've competed in a Science Olympiad, you may be used to these kinds of problems. Here are a few:

How many sheets of paper could be stacked from the floor to the ceiling in this room?

How many barbers are there in Chicago?

What is the mass of all automobiles scrapped this month?

The idea is not for you to come up with the right answer. The interviewer wants to see you reason your way through a problem. You'll have to start by making assumptions and estimates. You may be coached along the way, and you won't be penalized for guessing. You will be evaluated in terms of how well you respond to prompts, questions, and corrections. These interactions are an opportunity for a potential employer to see how you handle challenge.

Carol Dweck, in her book *Mindset,** shows the difference between a fixed mindset and a growth mindset. She did experiments where children were given hard problems. Those who had been told they were smart and led to believe intelligence was a fixed quality often gave up in frustration when they couldn't solve something right away. But those with a growth mindset, who had been praised for working hard and not giving up, greeted difficult problems with excitement.

If the thought of figuring out how many piano tuners there are in Rumford, Maine, fills you with fear and trembling, a job in which the interviewer asks a Fermi question may not be the right match for you. But if you can stay calm in the moment, say, "Let me take a minute to try to think this through," and then work with the interviewer, ask clarifying questions, and take feedback to stay on track, you will make a good impression and be more likely to land in the right place.

Interviews are opportunities for both parties to learn about each other. You are both trying to determine if it's a good match,

---

*Go to the library and check out Dweck's book. It's brilliant, readable and very helpful.

as in dating. Also, just as some people are awkward and uncomfortable having coffee with a stranger who may ultimately become their life partner, some interviewers are not very good at interviewing. This is all hard to figure out in the moment, so do your best and try to remain calm. I know, it's not easy.

While you can't expect the unexpected, there are some questions you absolutely have to be prepared to answer. And for those, you can prepare. What's the best way to do that?

Here's my advice. Practice for an interview by first writing the answers to questions you might expect.

You may protest that the job doesn't require writing. That may or may not be true, and I won't argue with you (though the fact is, most things require some amount of writing, and the better you are at it the easier your life will be). You may say you hate to write. This is true for many people.

I hope it takes some pressure off to know that only you will ever see what you come up with. Think of it as a job journal, like an old-fashioned diary that comes with a lock and a tiny key. Only you have the key. No one will judge your mistakes in grammar or point out hinky sentences. This is just a way to help yourself prepare. And preparation, if you haven't gotten the message by now, is essential if you want to be successful.

Here are some common questions you should be prepared to answer, even if you don't follow my suggestion to write them out:

Can you tell me a little about yourself?
How did you hear about this job?
Why are you interested in this job?
What would you say are your greatest strengths?
What do you think are your biggest weaknesses?
Give me an example of how you've worked through a
   problem/challenge/failure.

Practical Pro Tip: Write Out the Stories You Want to Tell in the Interview

Open a document and write me a letter (that you will never send) telling me any stories about yourself that might speak to the qualifications of a job you want. Don't sweat the writing, just get stuff on the page. See what you come up with. You may surprise yourself. In fact, you probably will.

Or perhaps you'll get stuck. You can't think of any examples of how you might fulfill the requirements. Ask people who know you well to tell you about yourself. Can they think of stories that will show how you are a good match for a job? Tell them the requirements and ask them to help you brainstorm. Parents may be an excellent resource here. But they might not have applied for a job in years and may not realize, unless they're involved in hiring, how things have changed. So listen to them, always, then make sure you also test things out with your network of unofficial mentors.

Eventually you will have a lot of words that tell a bunch of stories about you. You've gotten it all out. Clean up the writing. This is the long version of "About Me" that you can work from.

Now make a reverse outline. Go through and in all caps write a single sentence or phrase (the weekly dinner party; taking notes for Rachel's course) that identifies what the anecdote is and the skill it represents (collaboration; organization). Never delete anything from this long version.

Next, for each application go through the job description again and underline or highlight every requirement, skill, or qualification. Then make a copy of your long "About Me" and highlight each story that addresses that part.

Open a new document and, using the requirements listed for the job as your template, under each one map the phrase or sentence that reminds you of the story that addresses it. Practice responding to "Tell me a little about yourself" and use this document as a cheat sheet. It shouldn't sound rehearsed, but it will be better if you practice. You can even bring that document to the interview as long as you don't read from it. You could use it to refresh your memory just before you go into the interview room.

An unreasonable amount of work that could pay off

It's up to you to understand who you are, what you value, and how you want to spend your time. When you put effort into working on the response to a request to say who you are, you'll be doing something that will help you do more than just nail an interview. It will allow you to figure out some real and important stuff you may never have thought about explicitly.

When you go into an interview and it's clear you know who you are (as it relates to the job at hand), both you and the hiring manager will be better prepared to know if the relationship will work. The goal isn't just to get any job (though as the process drags on and your dad gets on your nerves it may feel that way). It's to get the right job at the right place that's the right match. Goldilocks may have been an entitled little brat, but we all want the same things.

Tell me about yourself

If you practice nothing else, please prepare to answer this seemingly easy question: *Can you tell me a little about yourself?*

What they're really asking is, of course, "How will hiring you make my job easier?" Of all the many things you could say about yourself, you must craft a narrative that shows why you are a good match for *this* job. You won't land a job by answering that you like piña coladas and getting caught in the rain.*

What will make you good at this job? What makes you a good contributor to this organization? You shouldn't discuss the time you won a spelling bee (unless you're applying to be a proof-

---

*If you're bored, google "Escape (the Piña Colada Song)" for a giggle. Or ask your parents or grandparents about it.

reader) or how you are one of eleven children (unless you can show this means you know how to work in groups that might not always get along). Instead, come up with what Hollywood calls an elevator pitch* for each job. A short, snappy statement that gives a good picture of who you are and why you are someone they would enjoy working with.

The key to success, again, is storytelling. Think of yourself as a character. We don't get to know our favorite fictional creations because the author has given us a list of abstract qualities. We get to know—and love—these fictional folks, who in the best books seem as real to us as family members, because we see them interact in situations that are challenging, or fun, or mundane.

Here's an example. I have a friend who tends to speak at high volume. If she claimed, "I'm the kind of person who has a loud voice," I wouldn't think much of it. The "I'm the kind of person" riff seems like a crutch. But in fact, what I've heard her say (loudly) is that she grew up in a family of girls close in age, all of whom wanted to be heard. They learned to shout over each other at the dinner table. If a job depends on your ability to make your voice heard in a noisy situation, this might be something worth mentioning. Especially if, in an interview, you show you have learned to modulate the volume.

Before you start writing your shitty-first-draft-eyes-only narrative, make a list, based on the job description, of what you think they're looking for.

Here's an example. For a job working as an admissions counselor at a large state university, the required qualifications listed— with the warning that these must be "demonstrated," mean-

---

*Because often all would-be filmmakers get to pitch an idea is the time it takes to ride an elevator from the lobby to some upper floor.

ing you have to find a way to show you really have done these things—are:

A bachelor's degree and one (1) year of student services experience; demonstrated experience working with diverse populations; excellent presentation abilities; oral and written communication skills; program or event planning abilities; computer skills, including proficiency with Microsoft Office Suite; a valid driver's license; being willing and able to travel and work some weekends/evenings.

When asked to talk about yourself, what can you say?

Even if you don't have experience directly related to student services, you could talk about clubs or organizations you joined that involved other students.

Think about your experiences with diverse populations. Did you have classes that included lots of nontraditional students who were much older than you? What did you gain from hearing about their experiences? Was there financial diversity? Did you struggle to pay for a night out when other students were spending hundreds of dollars a week on fancy caffeine delivery systems? Were you often the only [BIPOC, woman, queer person, diabetic, Jew] in a group? How did you share your culture [coming from a big Italian Catholic family, being a city kid without a driver's license, graduating from a high school with a class of seven] with students from different backgrounds? Think about situations in which you were with people who were other than you—whatever that might mean—and write an account. See what you say.

It will never be sufficient to claim you have excellent ability at oral and written communication. But you might say you took a class where the professor was brilliant but a little . . . well, let's just say organization was not her strong suit. So you offered to take notes in class and then post them online for other students. You created an Excel spreadsheet of projects, their due dates, and who needed to do what when.*

To be able to graduate from college debt-free, you had a job on the graveyard shift at a warehouse, so you're used to long hours.

While it might be nice to hear, eventually, what you like to read or that you're an ace at badminton, or how your little brother is annoying (but you still love him), none of that will be relevant to the job.

You should never be caught off guard in an interview when asked this obvious question. You will be asked. And you will be asked why you want the job you are applying for. I promise. After your thirty-eighth unsuccessful interview, you may have gotten a little better at answering, but why not set yourself up for success from the beginning?

And if you're interviewing for thirty-eight jobs at thirty-eight places, you need thirty-eight versions of your story. Just as you'll need thirty-eight cover letters and thirty-eight resumes. If you're thoughtful about your search instead of hitting Submit to every job you find that pays $100,000 and you take time to prepare for each one, I'm hoping you won't have to go to the thirty-ninth.

I suggest that for each of the questions you can expect to be asked—about you, about them, your strengths, your weaknesses, an example of a time you struggled—you write an answer, complete with at least one specific story, and then boil it down to a reverse outline so you're clear about the points each anecdote is making. Color-code it against the job description. Do this every

---

*Giant shout-out to the legions of students who have done this for me in every class, many of whom did such a terrific job I told them they could list "teaching assistant" on their resume.

time. Then boil it down to a few Post-it notes that you can put on your computer for ready reference during a video interview, or in a notebook you can review if you're on the phone.

What is your biggest weakness?

Most of us are better at noticing the good things about our friends and family than about ourselves. Sometimes we're more generous with them.

By the same token, it can be easier to find faults in others, even if we share the same flaws.

We all have weaknesses, imperfections, vulnerabilities: bad grades on our transcripts, a speeding ticket or two (or more), times we've spoken up when we should have remained silent and times we did nothing when a better person would have acted. No one is perfect, and most of us don't expect others to be.

A big mistake people make in writing, especially for high-stakes tasks like college application essays or job cover letters, is to burnish themselves to a high gloss that makes them seem without dents or dings. They learn how to humblebrag: "I'd be perfect if I weren't so modest."

No one roots for the kid who always shoots their hand up before the teacher has finished asking a question. The sports star who walks around like they don't know the name of the kid who raises their hand first is no more likable.

But it's hard not to feel compassion for the shy, quiet person who's afraid to ask their crush to the prom.

When we see honest vulnerability, we feel empathy.

And when we know and admit to our own faults, we can work to overcome them instead of papering them over with unfounded bravado.

A question you can expect is, "What is your biggest weakness?"

You'll find many people who tell you that the "right" answer is, "I'm a perfectionist." Excuse me, again, while I barf.

Now, this may be true for you. But if someone answered a question this way, I'd think she read on a website or in a book (not this one) that it's the thing to say. At this point, it's a freaking cliché. And though clichés become tired because they're so often true, that doesn't mean we should deploy them.

So it's incumbent upon you, perhaps with the help of friends and family, to think hard about your real weaknesses.

If you're a procrastinator, is it in your interest to try to change? If you say this about yourself in a job interview, people will think, *that may be fine if you work alone, but what if, as is often the case in jobs, other people are involved?* No one wants to risk a delay because you've missed a deadline. You can explain how you've come up with strategies to deal with your tendency to delay. Maybe you've learned to set your internal deadlines ahead of actual ones. Or you meet a friend at a coffee shop, where you sit across from each other and work.

Think of examples when you've gotten in your own way, then explain strategies you've found to help.

Maybe you tend to work quick and dirty, making lots of mistakes in your first attempts.* You've learned to allow yourself to create a mess in the first part of a project, give yourself lots of time, then you force yourself to go back and clean everything up.

The main thing is not that you don't have any weaknesses. We all have plenty, and pretending you're perfect won't fool anyone. The question to answer is how you deal with your real weaknesses and that you know what you need to be successful.

---

*Um, guilty, as the readers of the early drafts of this book well know. Thank goodness there are people willing to clean up my messes.

What are your greatest strengths?

This may be even harder to answer. Again, you'll need to find a story.

Instead of saying you like helping people, think of a time when you went out of your way to do that. Rather than claiming you never give up, talk about when you failed your first college physics test, then spent hours watching videos until you understood the concepts you'd missed in class. On your midterm, you earned a B-. But you felt you still weren't quite getting it, so you went to the professor's office hours each week, and she went over your tests question by question. You asked if she would give you extra problem sets so you could practice. You aced the final and ended the course with a B+ that you were very proud of.

Now, you may never have done that. But you've done other things that led you to say you never give up. What are they? Write out the stories so you'll be prepared to tell them in your interview.

Again, ask people for help. You may not know what sets you apart. Things you take for granted may in fact be remarkable.

Years ago, a friend told me a story about her son. He was born with a congenital condition that caused one ear to not develop; it was just a little nub on the left side of his head, and it didn't hear. When he was in high school, his parents found a plastic surgeon who could craft a prosthetic ear for him that would look "normal." They were all set to go ahead when the son said no. He wanted to wait until there was a surgery that would give him a working ear. He didn't care that what he had didn't look like other people's ears. He liked his weird little nubbin. He even shaved his head so as not to hide it.

Her son had no idea this attitude set him apart from other teens who cared about fitting in. After talking to a family friend who hammered home that he was not typical, he wrote his college application essay about his ear, and not only was he admitted, he was sought out by the dean, who remembered that essay and found it remarkable.

What's his strength? He doesn't mind looking different. It had never occurred to him to mention it.

Make sure you're answering the questions

Some managers are just not good or experienced at interviewing. As I've advised, list things you would like to talk about. Write long versions of those stories, then go back and make sure they reinforce what you want to convey. You will be asked some version of "Can you tell me a time when you had to deal with something difficult?" Hearing this for the first time while you're wearing uncomfortable clothes, dripping with flop sweat, across from a person or group of people who will be judging you, probably won't feel great. Prepare. Write it out. Practice with other people. The New York and New Jersey Port Authority's HR director Michael Watson says, "Be conscious of how much time you take to answer questions. You cannot spend ten minutes answering one question. Answers should be clear, but also concise."

If you're posed a question you don't know how to answer, say you need to think about it and ask if you can follow up. No one will fault an applicant for being thoughtful and needing a little time to come up with a solid answer.

Take out the trash talk

If you've had other jobs, summer work, or internships, you'll be asked about those. "Tell me what it was like to go on this trip to Guatemala." Or, "I see you worked in a potato-processing factory for two summers."

Here, focus on what you learned and what skills you acquired that you could bring to this job (being able to get along with a diverse set of coworkers; having to work long hours in difficult conditions; translating instructions into Spanish for those who didn't speak English).

Do not complain or blame. Do not say everyone else on the trip was a lazy piece of dog doo and that you had to do all the work while they sat around and drank beer with the locals. Do not say you were the only Spanish-speaker, so everyone depended on you, and it was a pain in the neck. Do not complain about leaders or bosses or others you felt were incompetent.

All of that may be true. You may have, in fact, done heroic work in the factory, processing three times as many spuds as anyone else. Talk about how you did that: explain that while the average worker processed twenty-five pounds of potatoes an hour, you were able to do seventy-five because you figured out a way to gather them up before they went onto the line. (I'm making this up.) Maybe other people eventually saw what you were doing and copied you. In that way, the whole plant became more productive.

What you don't want to say is that your boss never told you it would be more efficient to do it that way, and he laughed when he saw you carrying three buckets instead of one. That he screamed at the other workers or mocked them. Take responsibility for what you've done. When you point a finger at someone, remember there are three fingers directed back at you.

If you got a C on your transcript, don't say that the professor was a notoriously hard grader. Or that "everyone gets a C in organic chemistry." Provide explanations, but don't make excuses. Say you tried hard. You realized you were struggling to understand chirality and should have joined a study group earlier in the semester. When you finally did, it helped a lot, but it was too late to save your grade.

None of these situations is perfect. But everyone wants to work with people who learn from their mistakes. Blaming others when things go wrong is not an appealing trait for an employee. Or an applicant. Think about times you wanted to blame someone else. Now ask yourself what you could have done differently. Taking responsibility is one of the things that separates grown-ups from children. Or good people from jerks.

Don't come in and tell me what's wrong with our organization

You already know you need to do a lot of research about the organization. As much as you learn, there's way more you don't know.

If you come in and proclaim, based on a quick scan of the website and some reviews (likely written by disgruntled employees), "What you really need to do is X," you'll probably be thanked for your time and, if you listen carefully, hear either cackles of laughter or a big sigh of relief as you're shown the door.

At this point you don't know enough to know what the problems are. Once you've worked on the job for a while, you may come up with more efficient ways to peel a potato. But in the interview? You know nothing. You'll win zero points by telling an insider what you think they don't already know. If they ask for your opinion, give it as tactfully and respectfully as you can.

When hiring for a library job, Caitlin Wheeler said she had a candidate who talked about how, on a previous job, he was able to lay out successful solutions to problems. It was a smart way of showing he would push for the betterment of the institution. He said things that showed he planned to be a team player and gave examples of specific things he'd done.

Show you are someone who thinks critically and works for positive change. But be respectful and curious. Seek to learn more before you spout off. And please, don't spout off in the interview.

Make sure you're applying for the right job

Attorney Jay Manning shared a revealing story about a recent college grad who applied for a job at his environmental law firm. She was the child of immigrants, and everything in her materials showed a string of experiences connected to her passion for human rights. That came through in her cover letter and her resume, and the people who interviewed her said she was very impressive. She wasn't shy in telling what she cared most about. She said she was also concerned with environmental issues, but human rights work was her calling.

Unfortunately, the firm didn't do human rights work, and this young woman didn't make it to the final round of interviews. The hiring team thought she was terrific but felt she would have been a short-timer, getting good experience with them and then moving along. Being honest cost her the job, which she no doubt needed.

To me, there are several lessons here. The most obvious is to make sure you're applying for the right job at the right organization. Take the job description seriously and understand what the company is and what it does. As I've already said multiple times, you must tailor everything to potential employers and show how you can contribute to their work, not tell them your own goals and aspirations. If they don't align, don't apply.

The basis for a conversation will be what you put on your resume and write in your cover letter. Be prepared to talk about those. If everything you put forward leads toward work in a different field, it's up to you to show how those experiences translate.

If that impressive young woman's goal was to get a job at this firm—whose values she had researched enough to make it to the near-final cut—she could have taken a different approach. She could have related everything she did in her human rights work and argued that she could translate that energy to a different field. She could have acknowledged she hadn't yet had enough experience to know if environmental issues would engage her as much as human rights, but she was eager for an opportunity to learn.

Given how awesome this young woman was, it's possible a different set of people would have hired her. That could have led to a frustrating experience for her and for her employers. Or she may have discovered the firm was a great place to work. She might have brought a perspective appreciated by her coworkers and possibly, in the long-term, have influenced the kinds of cases the firm handled.

You can't fake a passion. But it's important to remember that our interests change over time and with exposure. If you want a particular job, you must convince people you really do want it.

You also need to make sure you're applying for a job you're able to do. As I've said before, many people recommend that you go after things for which you're not totally qualified. Then make an argument for yourself.

When I hear this, I can't but help think of the scene in the wonderful movie *Ladybird*.

LADYBIRD: "What I'd really like is to be on Math Olympiad."
COUNSELOR: "But math isn't something you're terribly strong in."
LADYBIRD: "That we know of yet."

I love the *yet* in this answer. In it are hopes and dreams and a belief in oneself. It also reflects that many young people don't realize how much it takes to get from here to there. A ton of work is required to get something you think you might like but don't have experience in or aptitude for. *Yet*. And also, it makes me think about who feels privileged enough to allow their reach to exceed their grasp. We should all be ambitious and believe we are worthy. Don't decide for a hiring manager that you're not qualified before you even give it a shot. You may be much more desirable than you realize. In fact, you probably are. It's possible to be too humble.

Be prepared to answer probing questions about what's on your resume

Your resume and cover letter will get you in the door. Once you're in the interview, you must be prepared to answer questions. Do not lie. Do not pad. The truth will come out, and everyone who's been around the block a few times is good at sniffing out falsehood or unearned bragging.

Mike Bergmann's training as a physicist makes him suspicious of anything scientists refer to as "hand waving"—basically using gestures or vague speech to show you understand something when in fact you really don't have a clue. His goal in the interview, he says, is to look for "veracity and enthusiasm." That you didn't have an important role in a project matters less than if you learned something by watching. But if you fudge the truth? Into the bin you go.

Expect an interviewer to go through your materials and see through anything that has even a whiff of inauthenticity. Remember the person who said he was responsible for "ensuring the cleanliness of kitchen utensils?" Washing dishes is hard work. It's boring. But it must be done.

And you can use that to your advantage. You might add that you listened to audiobooks so you could keep up with your schoolwork. Maybe you worked in the dish room with someone else, say an older man who had emigrated from Eritrea. You'd never even heard of that country before he spent hours telling you what life was like there. You gained an understanding of ethnic conflict you'd never considered.

If you're applying for a job that expects a GPA on your resume and you don't put it there, be prepared to say why. You might even list an overall GPA of 2.9 and then separate out the GPA for your major, which was 4.0. You can explain you had to take several courses in English, and since your first language is Chinese, writing the papers required was difficult. But as soon as you started taking upper-level physics courses, you thrived.

You may put on your resume that you started an investment club at your college. I would ask how many members there were and how you recruited them to join. Oh, it was just you and you were investing money you'd inherited from your grandma? That might be impressive if you could describe the strategies you used to pick stocks, but it isn't the same thing as starting a club.

Anything you put down that isn't true is likely to come back and bite you on the butt. Remember the dean of admissions at MIT who fabricated degrees on her resume decades before the truth came out. The truth will come out. Fact-checking is easy in the digital era.

Please don't tell me about your anxiety disorder in the interview

It's been common in recent years for students in my classes to introduce themselves with their diagnoses. Something like, "I'm J. I grew up near Seattle. I'm a senior creative writing major, and I suffer from anxiety and depression." Or "Hi, um, I am on the autism spectrum. Oh, my name is Abraham, but I prefer to be called Olaf, because in the Bible Abraham was a sexist oppressor. My pronouns are they and their."

First, people should absolutely be addressed in the ways they want. Many are not comfortable with their given name and start using a new one in college or when they go into a different venue. You just have to be careful if you apply for a job using one name and your college transcript and your recommenders all refer to you by another.

In your materials—cover letter, resume, job application—you might need to write the name that matches your driver's license and Social Security number, then put in parentheses what you would like to be called. Again, you want to be yourself—the best version of yourself for this job. You need to be comfortable.

But maybe not so comfortable that you unload a bunch of irrelevant personal information. At this point it's important to say which pronouns you use—you can volunteer them if you're not asked—but no one needs to know who you like to sleep with or other things about your identity that are not essential to the job. Also, when you're applying, avoid mentioning preferences that may be accommodated once you've proved your value but not before you're even offered a job.

For example, you may not like to get up early in the morning. What young person does? But saying you prefer not to start work until 10:00 a.m. when the office opens at 9:00 a.m. isn't a good move.

You might have learned in college that you work best wearing headphones. In some organizations, sitting at a desk with beats coming from your ear buds would be seen as a lack of collegiality. In other places it would be fine.

Community organizer Sabrina Mauritz says she doesn't care if people show up with a whole buffet of mental health issues. But mentioning them outside a specific context or not in response to a question would be strange.

She'll often ask, "What are your support structures? How do you take care of yourself? What do you need from a supervisor?

What kind of environment do you work best in?" She may not be able to accommodate every condition, but, she reports, being able to say what you need shows self-awareness. For example, perhaps you need to wear headphones because you suffer from an anxiety disorder.

Often people will say, "I work best in" certain kinds of circumstances. Or "I have a hard time in open spaces, and I do better with headphones on." The idea that someone knows what they need to take care of themselves is awesome. But no one wants to hear, "I can't do X." Especially if doing X is an important part of the job, like approaching strangers on the street to sign a petition or cold-calling on the telephone.

It's up to you to adapt to a work world. In a corporate office, if the culture is one where people are expected to work together and be "professional," putting in ear buds could be seen as an act of aggression.

I've heard many hiring managers complain about attitudes of entitlement. Millennials seemed to really irk their elders with talk of needing to leave work early to get to a yoga class or taking off lots of time to travel. Every generation complains about "kids today," and I'm not sure those avocado toast–eating, experience-seeking folks were any worse than members of Gen X or Baby Boomers. They just have different values and concerns.

Gen Z has faced challenges that are crippling to all of us. There are threats coming from everywhere—the environment, political madmen, a divided country, and nasty ever-changing viruses. We've all suffered from anxiety and depression at times.

Do not change or compromise your values or give up your identity or sanity-preserving measures to get a job. But you do have to find an organization, or at least a boss, that will allow you to work in ways that are comfortable and productive, and that means—here it comes again—finding a match that feels right.

As I've said, the job search is like dating. There are some people who share little personal information in the beginning of a relationship. They gradually get to know each other but still, even after they've been together for years, maintain a slight reserve. And there are those who, after the second date, pee with the bathroom door open. Some couples eat dinner each night with meat and three vegetables, sitting at a table with candles burning. Others are content to stand at the kitchen counter playing Bananagrams and noshing on a big bowl of buttery, salty popcorn.

There are no right and wrong ways to do stuff. These are not differences that show any kind of moral superiority. They're about knowing what works for you, what feels comfortable, and finding others who are happy to let you do your thing.

There are, of course, laws that protect groups that have traditionally been discriminated against, and your sexuality, race, and health issues are all things that cannot be held against you. Once you are employed, that is. It's hard to prove that you didn't get a job because in the interview you went on and on about your anxiety disorder. No one will say that's why they didn't hire you. When there are plenty of great candidates for every job, all employers need to do is say they found someone who was a better match.

The path of least resistance is to say no. Your goal in this (and in all situations where you want something badly) is to make it easy for the other person to say yes.

As you prepare for the interview, think about what's important to you in terms of your identity and work habits and preferences and see if there are ways you can convey those things without sounding like you're making a list of demands.

Although a friend of mine who works in corporate communications advised, "Please don't tell me about your anxiety disorder in the interview," I think you can find a way to mention things that may be difficult for you—especially if you add, "and here's how I deal with that." And, again, only if it's relevant to the job. If you feel you need to mention that you're on the autism spectrum, you can explain what that means: "Sometimes I may not be able to read social cues. So I ask people to clarify what they mean if I think I may be missing something." Or "Sometimes my feedback comes out sounding a little harsh. I've learned to encourage people to remind me to tell them what I think is good before I start criticizing. I appreciate the reminders."

If depression causes you to take several mental health days off from work, are there ways you can make up for them? Are you able to work through the night and on weekends to meet a deadline?

In college you can apply for accommodations that will help you complete your classwork. You can request distraction-free testing, extra time for assignments, bringing your support animal to class. Your professors want you to be successful and are willing to create an environment that will best allow you to learn. We're there for you (I hope that's been your experience). Just as your family was (I hope). Until this point, it's been all about you.

But when you sign on to work for an organization, you can't forget you're working *for* them. Everyone wants to keep good employees happy, and as you move along and prove your value, you'll be able to request things that may benefit lots of other people as well (a break room that has healthy snacks, including, naturally, Cheez-Its). But at the beginning of your career, no one owes you a thing, including accommodating your preference for listening to music while you work.

You've already learned as much as you could about the organization and the job before you got to the interview. Once you're there, you can ask questions that will help you determine if it's a job you really want.

The questions you ask

At the end of every interview, you will be asked if you have questions. You should have questions.

They should not include "What's the salary?"

One of the mistakes many job seekers make is to ask about money during the interview. You should have done enough homework to have some idea of what it will be. Until you get an offer, you're not in a position to negotiate.

Remember that when you are hired for a position, the organization will have to spend time and money to train you until you can become a valuable member of the group. Your first few weeks—or months—you will be a drain on resources. Unless you've been in the world in a similar capacity and have proved your worth, you're probably not in a great position to negotiate a higher salary than what's offered.

Another question not to ask: "When can I expect to be promoted?"

I told you early on in this book about a young person who, in an interview, asked, "Just for funsies, when could I expect to be promoted?"

He told his mentor this, and she advised him never to say "funsies"* in an interview and never to ask about money until he had a job offer in hand.

With coaching from her, he got a great job that would position him perfectly for the career in government he wanted. On his first day at work, he said he thought he should be paid more money than he'd been offered (and had accepted).

The next day, his second on the job, he was told that the posi-

---

*Unless you have a good idea of the organization's culture and how that would be received. In this case, interviewing with a conservative political group, it was a no-no.

Practical Pro Tip: Bring a List of Questions to the Interview

Based on the research you've done, make a list of real questions you have about the organization or the job. It's better to do this in advance so you can be thoughtful. When I worked in admissions, students would often ask me what I'd like to change about the university. While that might be a good question for a current student, it's a terrible one to ask an admissions officer. A better strategy might be, "What do students complain about because they don't understand how things work?"

Make sure your list shows that you've done research and aren't asking for answers you could have googled. Ask about career paths, interactions with other departments, and the organization's plans for the future. Keep your focus outward, not on yourself.

tion wasn't going to work out and they were going in a different direction.

Big humiliation, right?

This person spun the experience in the following way: he believed they had done him a favor. Being fired, he said, signaled it wouldn't have been the right workplace for him. It was clearly a toxic environment.

He thought the problem was them, not him.

It wasn't.

His mentor told me his attitude kept him from getting a number of jobs he wanted; he had ignored all her coaching.

I know you care about money and want to make as much as you can, especially if, like this young man, you come from a family that doesn't have much of it. But he made some easily avoidable mistakes.

Instead of asking when you can expect to be promoted, you can ask what the typical career path might be for someone starting in this position.

You can ask, "What's been the hardest thing in finding an applicant? Are there particular qualities or qualifications you're looking for?"

A hiring manager told me about a TikTok that gave the stupidest advice she'd ever heard. A young guy says he knows the best question you can ask in a job interview: "Do you have any hesitancy about hiring me?"

He claims the interviewer will say, "Nope, you're great." Or they'll give you feedback that will help in your next steps. Or, he says, you can argue with them.

Hiring managers seem to be split on whether this is, in fact, a good question. If you're applying for a sales job, Mikki Hubbard thinks it shows you're not afraid to do hard things.* Especially, she says, if it's done respectfully.

But what you think is reasonable and polite may look different to someone else. Instead of asking for direct feedback, it may be safer to keep things general.

Good questions show you've done research and are ready to do the job. Many managers have told me it's a real plus for candidates to bring a list of questions to the interview. It's not cheating; it's a way to show you care and you've prepared. You can ask something generic, like "What has kept you here for so long?" "What's your favorite memory from your time here?" And "What would my first thirty or sixty days look like if I were to get this job?"

You can also get specific, as would be appropriate for someone applying for a technical job. Max Mankin offers this:

> Show that you understand or want to understand how your function in the company interfaces with other functions. For instance, if you're applying for an engineering job, ask how the engineers

---

*That question, it turns out, is a pretty classic closing for sales calls. So, as is the case with everything in this book, much depends on industry practices, and it's in your interest to find out what those are.

in that group interface with product management, to make sure your technical work is something customers value. Another good question to ask is something like, "What is the business imperative for hiring for this role now?" Questions like these show you care about the broader company, not just your day to day work.

Legal recruiter Robin Schachter says, "There are ways to ask questions that demonstrate you understand you are there to make everyone else's job easier: What are the most important ways I can contribute in my first 60–90 days? What are the first projects I can help take off your desk? What are the best ways I can get a feel for how the team works so I can ramp up with the least amount of interruption? Other questions to come prepared to ask: What issues keep you up at night? What are things you wished you'd known about the company/job/industry before you joined? What do you read regularly to keep up with what's happening in the industry?"

You're not expected to know everything—or really anything— but it will go a long way if you're thoughtful and curious and ask good questions.

Practice, practice, practice: Do mock interviews with your toughest friends

Here's a story I've been thinking about ever since my friend told it to me. This friend is badass. She graduated from an elite university and got an MBA from another fancy-pants school. She comes from a family of achievers. She's one of those people who makes it look easy because she has confidence from a lifetime of success.

She was in New York City because her company, a very big company, was opening an outlet there and it was national news. She would be interviewed by the mainstream media about it.

Practical Pro Tip: Keep a Job-Search Log

Create a megadocument listing every job you've applied for, the names of every person you talked to, a list of the interview questions you were asked, and anything you feel went well or not so well. You can review this when you prepare for similar positions, or if the job you take doesn't work out (it happens) and you're on the market again.

The night before, she had dinner with an old friend and the woman's husband, whom she met for the first time. The husband worked for a famous anchorperson and had been in the news biz a long time.

When they sat down for the meal, my friend explained what she had to do the next day. The husband immediately offered to do a practice interview with her.

She said no.

He persisted and kept offering to throw some questions at her. She kept saying no; she didn't want to make him do work.

Even though she had gone through rigorous media training and had plenty of experience speaking to the press, she was nervous about the next day. But even more, she was embarrassed to do a practice in front of her friend. She was afraid of being judged.

Still, the husband started questions.

She felt uncomfortable at first, but it ended up going well. Because of that dinner, the next day, she nailed the interviews she had to do for real.

Her point in telling me this story is that it's important to practice for interviews. But I took away something else.

Even someone high on the food chain, with years of professional success under her belt, gets nervous. And she was embarrassed to practice in front of a person who already knew, liked, and respected her.

Find someone willing to give you a hard time

Jennifer Cast, an early employee at Amazon, says they often did "Rude FAQs." She says, "When you were getting ready to do media or be in an investment situation, you would meet with someone in PR who would ask you the hardest questions." What are the questions you don't want to answer? What will make you squirm? At Amazon, they would get trained doing that. They would, she says, get grilled. "You want to know when to stop talking. When to answer with a different answer. Prepare for the bump and run."

Years ago, a friend and I helped a Duke student, Lou, prepare for medical school interviews. I'd been his admissions officer and got to know him when he showed up on campus. My friend Andrew, a psychiatrist, had hired him for a work-study job and listed him as a coauthor on two medical journal articles. Lou was a great person and an impressive med school candidate. But we wanted to prepare him for hard interview questions.

One of the few blemishes on his transcript was a C in organic chemistry. I knew Lou wouldn't want to talk about it, so I asked, "Why did you get a C in org chem?" We broke him down (I think he started crying). Then we built him back up and helped him figure out how to respond. He's now a neurologist in Boston.

I also did a mock interview more recently with the friend of a friend, a middle-aged man, who was applying to veterinary school.

He talked about how, having been in the working world for so long, he was better qualified than others applying. He kept referring to fellow applicants as "kids," and the condescension in his attitude made him unappealing.

After I asked him a bunch of questions, I reminded him it's

harder to get into vet school than into medical school, and those "kids" have all worked their butts off to get great grades so they could enter a field offering salaries meager compared with what human doctors command. And as much as he loved working with animals, as a vet his clients would be people, and he'd have to get along with them. Plus, I said, it's mostly women who go into veterinary medicine these days. That means that as a man he'd have an admissions edge, but anyone who came across as a big mansplainer might not be the most attractive student or peer.

He had spent most of the time talking about the other applicants and not about why he wanted to be admitted or what he could contribute to the class. Once I pointed this out to him—which, yes, was a little ouchy—he was able to think harder about how he presented himself. He got in.

If (when) you mess up

In situations where we are anxious and feel pressure to do well, we often mess up. At least I do. What happens if you say the wrong thing? What if, even after I'd told the vet school candidate I think it's dismissive to use "kids" about people who will be his peers, it just slipped out?

At some point, either at the end of the interview when asked if there's anything he wanted to add, or even just a few moments after the k-word escaped his mouth, he could say,

> You know, I'd like to clarify something I said. I used the word "kids" because I'm a little self-conscious about my age. I know younger applicants have the advantage of being used to being in school, and it's a long time since I graduated. The fact is, I'm a bit intimidated by them, so it's easier to think of them as kids than as the academic superstars I know they are. I'm happy to be in the

minority here, as a man and an older student, and in that way I hope to bring some diversity to the class. I'm eager for the opportunity to learn and grow.

If you say something that didn't come out quite right or see that the interviewer took it in a way that didn't convey your real meaning, it's okay to back up and ask for a moment to think about how you want to rectify the situation. Then, clarify and explain.

Every employer knows human workers will make mistakes. How you respond when you screw up is what they really want to know. That's why you can expect a question asking for an example of a time you failed. It's not the failure, it's your *response* to it that counts.

You can also follow up by sending a message as part of your thank-you note (more on that in a later chapter) and say, on reflection, you'd like to clarify something you said in the moment.

Quick Takes

- It's completely normal to be nervous about your interview.
- Keep your phone close, and check your email regularly before and after the interview.
- Be prepared to say why you're interested in the organization and the position.
- Keep notes with specific questions and information you'd like to convey during the interview.
- You don't have to bring your whole self to work; be the best version of yourself for that job.
- Don't let your online interview venue be the reason you don't get the job.
- Make sure to listen attentively.

- Interviews are opportunities for both parties to learn about each other.
- Prepare, prepare, prepare.
- Find someone willing to give you a hard time in a practice interview so you're physically and mentally prepared.
- Understand who you are, what you value, and how you want to spend your time.
- Don't complain about other jobs or bosses.
- Anything that isn't true is likely to bite you on the butt.
- You should have questions.
- If you mess up, what matters is how you respond.

8 References

Ask before you list

You don't need to give up precious real estate on your resume to list references. No one expects that. Checking up on what other people say about you comes much later in the process.

However, as recruiter Wenda Cenexant says, "Have references ready and informed that you're job-searching ahead of time. Speed is the top thing. The thing is not to have hiring managers waiting. Be as proactive as possible."

As with everything else in the job search, your references need to be relevant for the job you're applying for. Longtime executive Ellyn Foltz says, "Please do not give me the person you babysat for, your minister, your pediatrician. You're wasting my time, and I will question your discernment."

Determine who can speak to your ability to do the job. If it's a technical job, a chemistry professor makes sense. An art teacher, not so much. Best are former employers or managers at internships who can speak to your work ethic and ability to accomplish tasks.

No one checking references wants to call someone and hear them say, "Oh, they used me as a reference?" Always ask permission and let references know exactly which jobs you're applying for and why. While you can't control what people say about you,

you can help them give you not just a positive recommendation, but a good one. There's a difference. A reference might say you're a wonderful person, but it won't matter much if they have no idea what the job is and what skills it will require. Guide them by saying, "Here's why I want the job, and I'd like for you to be able to speak to [these things you know I've done under your guidance]." Many places will interview only people whose references say they are good or excellent.

Whenever a student asks me to write a letter of recommendation or to serve as a reference, I ask them to show me their cover letter, resume, and the job description, and to write me a letter. Over the years, I've had a lot of students, and while some stand out, I don't always remember specific things they've done. The more information I have—especially details that jog my memory—the better I'll be able to support them.

In fields that are small worlds, like the kind of community activism Sabrina Mauritz does, she says, "A personal reference from someone I respect in the field counts a lot to me. I almost couldn't care less about how crappy your cover letter or resume is." And she means it.

She says, "Someone I hired sent me a really bad cover letter and resume—it could have been for retail as well as for my [organizing] job—but they had a reference from someone I really respected. The person who was a reference actually told me about experiences the applicant had that were very relevant and important that they didn't even think to include in their resume and cover letter."

Now, at this point I hope you know enough not to write a crappy cover letter or resume, but a good reference can save you from the bin if the person is someone the hiring manager knows.

As I've said, many big corporations give referral bonuses to

Practical Pro Tip: List Your References

Make a list of your references with their current contact information. Each time you apply for a job and get to the point where you're asked for references, send each person a brief note, a copy of your cover letter, and the job description. This way they'll be prepared to respond, and you'll give them yet another reason to sing your praises. Then thank them and let them know the outcome. You may need their help again.

employees who help them find good workers. This is where networking skills can pay off. Approach the folks you've been chatting with on LinkedIn and, after you've made a good impression, you can ask if they'd be comfortable submitting your resume for a job at their organization.

On a separate document (you will submit only when asked for it), do obvious things, like making sure you have the correct spelling of names, current addresses and titles, a phone number that doesn't go to the local pizza place, and some context about why you included them as a reference.

There are different ways of thinking about ordering the list. Some say you should put the best, most relevant person at the top. Others suggest listing all references in alphabetical order by last name to avoid any kind of bias. If the first one or two references are positive, many employers will simply stop calling. You can have three to five if you make sure they all know you're listing them and what position you're applying for.

It's important to ask someone explicitly if they feel they can provide a positive recommendation, or if they think you should approach someone else. Most people will say yes if asked, but there are plenty of ways to give lukewarm references that don't

**Practical Pro Tip: Make Sure You're Using
the Right References for Each Job**

Use your board of directors to ask about the appropriateness of a
reference. You may have adored a professor and done well in his
class, but he won't be able to speak to what it's like to have you as
an employee. Put a star beside the name of any of your contacts
who might be able to serve as a reference. Again, this is where it's
helpful to have their information (phone numbers, addresses) in
one place.

do a candidate any good. Make sure you can gauge their enthusiasm for the task.

And since these are, presumably, people who know you in a
professional context, you can exploit them for all they're worth.
What I mean is, you can ask them to help you prepare. Ask what
they think your strengths are. What do they think you need to
work on? Do they have advice about how to highlight certain projects you've done (things they may find impressive and you just
think, *What? That? That was no big deal*). Ask them to read your
cover letter and resume, and listen to everything they say. If you
don't agree with a suggestion, thank them for their time and then
check with someone else about it. Remember the Ben Franklin effect. Asking for help—as long as you do it in a way that is respectful of their time and allows them an easy out—will generally get
people on your side.

On my favorite TV show, *Project Runway* (and more recently,
Making the Cut), Tim Gunn is the world's best, most supportive mentor. His feedback is smart and rarely hurtful (well, one
time he told a contestant the dress he'd designed looked like it
was being attacked by birds). But if he puts his fist to his chin and

says, "I'm concerned," oh, boy. That means there's a big problem. Generally he gives broad advice that lets the designer know what the issue is, and while he may offer a specific suggestion on how to solve it, he wants the contestants to follow their own vision.

Good designers, those who go on to win and become successful, listen hard when Tim puts hand to his chin and says, "I'm concerned." They start over, or they make big changes. Arrogant contestants, who believe they know more than they do, ignore him. Then, once their designs are on the runway, the judges complain about exactly the problem Tim identified. But by then it's too late.

These are the Teflon people. Nothing sticks to them. I can tell you they're not much fun to have as students. As employees, they tend to be giant pains in the butt. Tim once said to a contestant, "I can't want this for you more than you want it." I quote that all the time to people who don't seem hungry enough.

Conversations with references can be a chance for you to get— and hear—real feedback. If someone looks at your resume, cocks their head, and says the equivalent of "I'm concerned," listen. Don't get defensive or try to explain your reasons. Hear what the problem is and fix it.

Your references are—or at least should be—people who are already on your side and want you to succeed. Take advantage of them and ask for their help. No one will begrudge you this because it will be easy for them to give you quick feedback and, well, everyone likes to feel their advice is valuable.

Quick Takes

- **Have references ready and informed that you're job hunting ahead of time.**

- Ensure all the information presented for each job reference is current, correct, and relevant.
- Waive your right to read written recommendations.
- A personal reference from someone in the field counts a lot.
- Remember that everyone will gladly listen to someone they trust. So put in the work to cultivate good relationships.

9 *Following Up*

Manners matter

Your family probably told you to send thank-you notes when you received a gift. Sometimes you did, sometimes you didn't. Your grandparents and Auntie Rachel still love you. But there's no excuse for not taking every opportunity to make a good impression on a future employer.

It seems obvious, but people still sometimes need to be prompted to always send a follow-up note. It doesn't require much more than "Thank you for taking the time to talk with me. I know you're busy and I learned a lot." For jobs, you could add, "If I have the opportunity, I think I would be a good match, and believe I could contribute over time."

Even better is to mention something specific you learned in the interview or conversation: "I so enjoyed hearing your theories about why rats are the perfect pets for city people, and I'll be able to use the examples you gave me when I interview for jobs at animal shelters."

Don't wait too long. Mikki Hubbard says, "You should follow up within twenty-four hours with anyone you spoke with. Whoever set up the interview should be able to get you emails for the members of your interview team. And you can ask to connect on LinkedIn. That's another opportunity to say thank you in a timely basis."

Ellyn Foltz recommends something even better: "I like people

Practical Pro Tip: Send Fan Mail to Authors of Books You Like

You know what's almost as hard as finding a job? Writing a book. Authors love to hear from readers. Most of them won't be able to help you, but you can make their jobs easier if you offer morsels of praise. We're all insecure messes (in author Louise Penny's acronym, we're all FINE ["Fucked up, Insecure, Neurotic, and Egotistical"]), and every nice word helps (racheltoor@gmail.com). Just saying.

that send me an email with an idea that occurred to them after the interview. They can just say, 'It occurred to me that I would really like to work for you, so I went back and read an article.'" The idea of following up goes beyond just thanking them for their time. It's another chance to say why you think you're the right person and why is this the right place for you. Ellyn loves people who say, "Here's an idea I have for if/when I start working for you." She says it's an imaginative step of seeing yourself in the job. And that helps her see how you will be able to contribute.

What if you thought the interview went well but still didn't land the job? You're flummoxed and wonder what went wrong. It's a dicey proposition to ask someone for help if they're not going to hire you, but if you feel a real connection, you can reach out and ask if they have time and are willing to give you some critical feedback. You might find you did something unintentionally rude, or you seemed like a great person, but they decided to go with someone else. I wouldn't recommended doing that at the end of an interview; that would feel awkward. But you could wait a few days after hearing back and send a quick, polite email asking if they could tell you anything that would help you in your job search.

To such a request, Sabrina Mauritz says, "I will respond if I have a connection—if I say I hope you will apply for future positions I really mean it. If I just say I wish you luck, I don't care if you apply again. Most of the time it will be there's just someone else stronger."

She adds that if a candidate follows up and sounds genuinely enthusiastic, as if they listened and are eager, that might just get them a second interview.

The main thing is to be respectful of everyone's time. Busy people are eager to get the hiring process over with once they find the right match. And always be polite.

I know you know this. Kind of. Still, I'm often surprised when I've gone out of my way to do a favor for someone and they never acknowledge it with a quick "thanks." Next time I might be a little less inclined to help them.

Offers! $$$! Bennies!

If all goes well, you'll end up with one or more offers. Even if an offer seems great, it's a good idea not to accept immediately. Johan Zhang, who dropped out of Harvard to found a successful start-up, advises when you get an offer, "Express excitement and gratitude for the opportunity, and politely let them know you would like some time to review the offer. Maybe clarify the deadline when they need to hear back. Hang up, clear your head, talk to family/friends, etc. Then decide whether you would like to negotiate for more." He says he's noticed what stops young people from doing this is the fear the offer will somehow disappear. Or they don't feel they're "worth it" to begin with and it's ungrateful or rude to ask for more. In reality, employers expect you to be thoughtful, so don't throw away your shot to think about what you want.

There is plenty of advice available on negotiating, and you can google to see what kind of salary you can expect. You'll have to research which parts of the job are negotiable, which are fixed, which are flexible, and why.

Asking for more money by saying you simply want more is not a good strategy. You need to offer a reason. Perhaps you have data from online sources showing others in that position are being paid more. Or better yet, perhaps you have another offer in hand from a different company that is paying more. Johan advises, "A classic line is, 'I have an offer from this other company which is paying me $30 an hour. However, I would much prefer to work at your company because of reasons A B C (great culture, amazing team members, mission). Would you consider matching the rate to make the decision easier for me from a financial perspective?'" It's always great to secure more than one offer to increase your negotiating leverage. But for the love of all that is good in the world, please don't lie.

And don't go into "fight mode" during negotiations. What Johan has seen working with recent grads is that "whether due to nervousness or incorrect preconceived notions of what a 'negotiation' is via movies and TV, applicants can sometimes develop a 'me vs. them' mentality, as if they're in a battle with their employer." An adversarial tone is not a good way to start a relationship. The employer is not out to get you and pay you as little as possible. If you feel like they are, run. Seriously. If you've been polite and respectful but feel you're not being treated the same way, pay attention, and think about whether you might be entering a bad relationship. No job is worth that. You will find something else, something better.

You will want to advocate for yourself, always with respect, and remember this is a conversation about what it will take to get you to join the team. It's possible you will be offered a lower-level job than the one you applied for. This can feel disappointing but could turn into a win. I know many people who started as assistants and quickly rose through the ranks. When I worked in publishing, I was one of them. Once you're in the door and prove your worth, you may be promoted quickly.

Remember, if you come in with little or no direct work experience, you'll log time in the liability column before being switched over to the assets. Organizations must invest in training you.

But you get to make the final decision. Always remember during the process that you are not just desperately trying to get a job.* Interviews are two-way streets, even if the traffic may be heavier in one direction. You are evaluating whether this job, at this organization, will be a good match for you.

Take notes on your impressions. Was there something in your initial interview that felt a little off but that you may forget about or overlook when an offer is forthcoming? Did the man you'd be working for call you "Sweetie"? Did it seem like everyone in the office could have performed in a zombie movie? Were expectations made clear, or did they keep throwing up additional hurdles for you to hop over? What was the turnover in your position? Did people stay for decades, or was it a revolving door of assistants? Were you asked about your tattoos and piercings in a way that made you feel uncomfortable, or were they seen in a good way?

It's in no one's interest for you to take a job and realize in a few weeks or months that it's not the right match. We all make mistakes, and you shouldn't work at a place that feels hostile. Although most of us don't stay long at our first jobs, it won't look great on your resume to have short stints at several places early in your career unless you can give good reasons for the moves. And whenever you leave a job, it's best—though not always pos-

---

*Even though you may feel this way. While eagerness is an attractive quality, desperation is not.

sible—to do it on friendly terms and make sure you'll get a good reference.

Quick Takes

- Send a thank-you note. Best if you mention something specific discussed during the conversation or mention ways you're currently working to be better equipped for the job.
- Take notes on your impressions. Remember to conduct your own assessment as well. Don't ignore any red flags or anything that doesn't sit well with you about the organization or its people. Your goal is not just to get a job but to find one where you're comfortable and most likely to grow as a person and an employee.
- When you get an offer, you can ask for time to think it over.
- It's fine to negotiate, but remember that you will be working together to find a solution rather than engaging in salary warfare.

10 *The Long (Long, Long) Haul*

I started this book by describing a fictional hiring manager named Olivia. Now I want to tell you about a very real chef named Rachel.*

Chef Rachel went to culinary school instead of college, worked for some years in various kitchens, then started her own catering company. Just before the pandemic, she had some big business losses (not her fault) and decided to shutter her company. It was exhausting, and she was also doing a lot of gig work—teaching, consulting, special events. She wanted a more reliable source of income with less stress and fewer hours.

She knew it would take six months to a year to find a job and settled in for a long haul. She began sending direct messages on social media to people from culinary school. She used LinkedIn to connect with those she hadn't spoken with in twenty years. To each person she contacted she explained she had been running a small business for x years that had x employees and brought in x amount of revenue, but she was now ready to explore other opportunities. She asked about the companies they worked for, about their jobs, and whether they'd be willing speak to her.

---

*It's kind of annoying that she shares my name, but since this book is nonfiction, I won't change it. In my circle we call her "Chef Rachel" since I am the OG Rachel.

She approached the process as a research project and kept careful notes.

Chef Rachel went on a number of what she called "bogus interviews" for real jobs she didn't want. She knew she needed practice and figured it would be better to do that when the stakes were low. In that way she got a good idea about what compensation she could expect at different kinds of organizations and what perks were negotiable and what were not, then started narrowing down the kinds of places she thought would be a good match for her values and work style.

The people in her growing network were helpful and generous. One friend said she really should talk to Iris, who was great at thinking about this kind of stuff. In a ten-minute phone call, Iris asked her some questions that, Rachel said, changed everything. *What are you good at? What's your goal?* And, for the right position, *What are you willing to compromise on?*

She had begun to wonder if she had any transferable skills. In a ten-minute conversation, Iris was able to help Chef Rachel realize how much she had to offer and to think about ways to translate what she'd done as a chef into other capacities. For example, because she had also worked as a bread baker, Chef Rachel knew how to develop recipes by weight, not volume. That meant she knew how to scale—a transferable skill. Iris suggested she might be happy working in meal-kit development. Meal kits had become big business, and chefs were hired to do menu innovation. It had never occurred to Rachel this could be a good job for her, and she was intrigued. She told Iris she appreciated the conversation and hoped she would keep her in mind if anything came up. Then Chef Rachel kept networking. And working.

A few months later she heard from Iris. Someone she knew at a medium-sized meal-kit company was looking for a chef. Iris gave him Rachel's name, he called her, and they had a good conversation. He told her when she was ready to apply, she'd have to submit her resume through a website. When she'd done that she should notify him, and he'd have Human Resources search for it just in case she got screened out by the bots.

Studying the description, Chef Rachel realized what the job was really about: this was an e-commerce company. It was a start-up with a fast-paced culture. Sure, the product was food, and Chef Rachel knew food, but she also knew about launching a business. She was able not just to talk about what she liked to cook but to explain she understood the challenges this company faced and how she could contribute to their mission.

Bingo. Six months after starting her job search, Chef Rachel was hired.

When she told me all this I said, "Did you read my [not yet published] book? You did everything right!"

She said yeah, it worked out.

Then I asked how her experience of job searching had gone.

It was, she said, awful.

It was exhausting and demoralizing, and she was doing all this while also running her own business, keeping the imminent closure secret from her employees, and often having to do informational interviews from her car, which served as her office. The whole thing had been an ordeal. I asked how she'd stayed sane. She said she knew it would eventually work out and she was used to doing hard things. A friend reminded her if she landed at a place she didn't like, it didn't have to be forever.

Chef Rachel had a string of successes to look back on to keep her buoyed, but the job search is hard for everyone.

I hope you'll read this book, do everything the experts and hiring managers say you should do (and make none of the common mistakes I've described), and quickly get the first job of your dreams, where you'll have a wonderful and supportive supervisor who will teach you a lot and give you additional responsibilities that you'll find delightfully challenging, get promotions and raises, and have a fulfilling and happy work life.

However, it may not happen like that. This process can take a long time. You'll have to talk to a lot of strangers and submit many applications. You need to do everything you can to avoid burnout. Glenn Gutmacher says, "This is a numbers game. Don't give up—realize whatever number you're going to need and multiply it by ten." If you think you will have to apply only to five jobs, realize it may be more like fifty. And yes, each of those cover letters and resumes must be tailored to the job and the organization, so that's a lot of research.

Keep networking. This is how you'll learn about jobs. And it's also a way to keep yourself motivated and energized. Let the members of your network know what you're doing. Once someone is invested in you, they'll be happy to hear about any successes—or even near misses. When people write to me to ask for help, I always tell them to send me updates, and I mean it. I want to hear from them for years to come. And I'll take real pleasure in learning about their success.

The more effort you put in, the better your chances will be

As I've said, applying for a job may be the hardest job you'll ever have. Getting work—the right work—takes work. It can be a long haul. Frustrating. Demoralizing. The process can take weeks, months, even a year. The longer it drags on, the less energy and enthusiasm you'll have for the task. After the freedom of college, you may be tired of living back at home and hearing your dad tell you to pick up your socks or your mom asking how it's going and looking worried/pissed off. If your family struggles financially, you may have to take on a minimum-wage job, live in close quar-

Practical Pro Tip: Stay Sane by Doing Things You Love

It's easy to be consumed by a process that can take longer than you want and at times can feel demoralizing. Make a list of things that make you happy. It could include cuddling with your dog, baking brownies for friends, running up and down a mountain, taking bubble baths, drinking cheap whiskey, Zooming with a friend who moved across the country. Whatever. When we get depressed or demoralized, it can be hard to remember what we love. Having a list that reminds you and keeping it in plain sight can help. Doing those things will help even more.

ters, sleep on a sofa, and worry about the next meal. I know, this is hard stuff.

Even if you're amazing, and I'm pretty sure you are, the whole business of getting a job may not come easily. This may be the first time you feel like you're not getting what you want. That's because, as I've been hammering into you, what you want is no longer the most important thing. I'm always surprised when students are eager to leave the collegiate nest and start working in whatever they think the Real World is. Because, friends, the Real World is no picnic.

The more effort you put into finding a job, the more likely you are to find the right one. While I've used the analogy of dating, here's another: To me, it's more like training for a marathon. This is another area in which I have vast experience.

To finish a marathon, you must know what you're capable of and set a goal that's realistic, if ambitious, given where you're starting from.

Humility counts. You can wish for whatever you want, but you can't underestimate how hard it is to run 26.2 miles.

You must want it enough to work for it—going to the track when you don't feel like it and slogging through long runs in the cold/heat/rain/snow when you're tired.

You have to train smart. Many new runners do too much too soon and end up injured. You need to be astute enough to know how much you don't know, and to seek help when you need it.

You can't expect to wake up one morning having done no training and try to race 26.2 miles. You may be able to make it to the end, but it won't be pretty. And you may never want to run again.

But if you train well, you should be able to toe the starting line on marathon day and predict your finishing time, plus or minus a couple of minutes. Of course things can always go wrong. You could have eaten too much spaghetti at the prerace dinner and suffer from stomach cramps.* It might just not be your day. But your chances of achieving what you set your sights on go way up if you keep in mind what you need to do to get to the finish line. If you can muster a winning combination of respect for the distance, hard work, and a smart race strategy, you'll wear that finisher's medal with earned pride. Humble, hungry, and smart is the way to go.

Friends, you will get a job

The search process may feel draining. You'll need to find things to nourish and sustain you, whether that's going for a walk with friends or cuddling with your cat while you read a fantasy novel. It's normal to feel discouraged in the face of rejection. The whole thing may take longer than you'd like, and you may not find the perfect match at first. Your boss could be a jerk. So you'll apply for

---

*I can tell you that after having run seventy to eighty marathons and longer races, "carbo-loading" the night before a race makes zero sense.

another job. Everything you've learned from this book will help you. You'll know more, have experience to draw on, and have a bigger skill set.

Quick Takes

- If you get stuck, seek feedback on what you might be doing wrong.
- Find things to keep you happy (or at least less discouraged).
- Psych yourself up. The job-hunting process can get frustrating and might take longer than you'd expect.

One Last Thing: My Little Bag of Writing Tricks

My book *Write Your Way In: Crafting an Unforgettable College Admissions Essay*, contains pretty much every single thing I know about writing well in the first person.* Even though that publication is geared toward high school students, it includes my tips and practices to help you make a persuasive case for yourself and to sound like an appealing human on the page.

As with admissions essays, the key to good cover letters and resumes is to convey information—and personality—concisely. That's hard to do.

Pages ago, I promised I'd provide tools to put flabby prose on a diet. I gave an example of an opening line: "I am writing to you because I am very interested in applying for the position as an entry-level dog stylist at *Woofus* and I am attaching my resume to this message."

Then I suggested replacing that bloated version with this: "Attached please find my resume for an entry-level dog stylist position at *Woofus*," reducing the word count from 32 to 14.

What magic did I perform to make those extra words disappear?

Well, I'll show you. But first, a warning: if you're expecting

---

*So, it's a short book! Hahaha!

elaborate explanations about the principles of grammar and in-structions on how to diagram a sentence, you might want to find yourself a nun.* I'm just going to share my little bag of tricks in ways that make sense to me.

You need to keep in mind how hard it is to write concisely and still retain your own voice and unique perspective. That means every word has to earn its keep by doing some kind of work. Otherwise, out it goes.

So, which words get the boot?

To be or not to be

An easy trick to make prose concise (and livelier) is to go on a search-and-destroy mission for forms of the verb *to be*. They are *be, am, is, are, was, were, being, been*. To be clear, there's nothing wrong with these words—Where would we be without them?—but they're static. They don't *do* anything, which is, after all, the main job of a verb. *Action!*

If you look to replace them, you'll find stronger choices and make your prose more concise. If you search our flabby sentence above for *am* you would find, "I *am* writing because I *am* apply-ing for a job" you could say instead, "I would love the opportunity to work for you." True, it's the same number of words, but *love* is better than *am*. Am I right? If I were writing this, I'd use a contrac-tion and make it "I'd love to work for you," and I wouldn't end the sentence there. I'd add a *because* and say why. That way I shift the focus off me and what I want, and onto them. (This has been my main argument throughout the book, remember?)

---

*People who went to Catholic schools seem to know this stuff. One of my literary heroes, Joan Didion, wrote that grammar was a piano she played by ear. Me too.

Ing-ing

Notice I kicked to the curb all those words that end with -*ing*. These are not the toughest kids on the playground. I search my complete drafts for -*ing* and make sure I really want each word and can't find a better one. "I write" is better than "I am writing." That -ingy, -singy ending draws things out unnecessarily.

This, that, and there

When I finish a draft, I search for *this*, *that*, and *there*. There are reasons for this seemingly elaborate process that I go through. In a shitty first draft, my goal is to get everything onto the page. I need to see what I say. Then—and this is the fun part—I take pleasure in cutting. Searching for *this*, *that*, and *there* helps. I'll show you how.

Let's look at what I just wrote: "*There are* reasons for *this* seemingly elaborate process *that* I go through."

You probably read right over that. Nothing amiss. If you ask someone to proofread it for errors, they may not make a mark. You might expect that I'm going to tell you my reasons, so telling me that they exist (*there are*) is unnecessary. So, you'll get, "My reasons for this . . ."

But the *this* just reminds you I have a process. "Seemingly elaborate" may or may not apply. You decide.

That is a tricky one. Often I include it in an early draft because my ear likes the way *that* sounds. Usually it's not necessary for clarity. So "My reasons are that" is no better than "My reasons are," and if you're trying to cut words, the *that* can go. In cover letters and resumes, space is valuable. In longer pieces, you may want your prose to sound a certain way and like you (the best, smartest version of you). Make a deliberate choice each time you use *that*.

Something else to search for: prepositions. I learned what a preposition is in seventh grade from a teacher who used the example of Horatio the mouse. A preposition is anything Horatio could theoretically do with a desk. Horatio could go up, down, into, around, or through the desk. (He had superpowers, that mouse.) So I could get rid of that whole business of saying that this is a process *that I go through*. It's just my process. (I could also have written at the beginning of this paragraph: "Something else to search.")

I think of unnecessary prepositions this way. You can say I stood *up*. But standing implies up. Same with sitting *down*. I stood. I sat. Fewer words. Same meaning.

Let's go back to the sentence I started with in an admittedly tortured explanation, which you've probably forgotten by now: *There are reasons for this seemingly elaborate process that I go through.* The condensed version could read: *My reasons include brevity and clarity.* See? There's the beef! I didn't even have *brevity* and *clarity* in that original version. Now there's some substance to that first airy sentence.

Now, lots of books will give you reasons for what I've just said, but that's not going to come from me. Every time I'm on a chairlift (I don't love to ski, but I go sometimes), I always ask the person next to me to give me three things to think about as I'm making my way down the hill. It's not all that complicated, but each person gives advice differently. Some will say "use your edges," while others advise you to "carve with your big toe." The mechanics are identical, but some explanations hit me harder. At the end of this chapter I'll provide a list of resources if you're a giant nerd and want to get better at writing.* You find those that speak in a language you like to hear.

It

It is not specific. See what I mean? Usually you can find a noun to replace something vague that you refer to as "it."

Agency

In history classes (and others, I hope) teachers advised you to acknowledge agency. In class I once caught myself saying about Ukraine, "When the war broke out." I immediately called attention to my error. The war didn't break out. *Putin* invaded Ukraine. And *your excellent professors* advised you about the problems that arise when you gloss over agency in your writing: it lets the bastards off the hook and doesn't give heroes (like your teachers) credit.

You may have been taught about the active versus the passive voice, but that's more complicated. The bottom line: try to include action figures in your prose—people doing things, not just stuff happening (unless it's the weather).

Quantify, don't qualify

Especially in resumes, you need to quantify, not qualify, your experiences. Here's what Strunk and White's *The Elements of*

---

*By now I think you know me well enough to know (1) I want you to want to get better at writing because I think that will lead to success in whatever you do and (2) if you're a giant nerd, I love you.

Style[*] says about words called "qualifiers": "*Rather, very, little, pretty*—these are the leeches that infest the pond of prose, sucking the blood of words. The constant use of the adjective little (except to indicate size) is particularly debilitating; we should all try to do a little better, we should all be very watchful of this rule, for it is a rather important one, and we are pretty sure to violate it now and then." Now do you see why I love that book? Search for every *very* and *really* and destroy them. In Strunk and White's terms, "Omit needless words."

-ly

Not all adverbs end in -*ly*, but I can quickly and easily and happily and fancifully tell you that those that do are best tossed in the compost bin. I'll skip and dance to show you why they are less effective than using strong verbs like *skip* and *dance*. Good writing is specific and vivid. You want to give the reader a mental picture.

Clichés, word packages, junk phrases

You know what clichés are, and you all use them all the time. They come trippingly to the tongue and don't require work to visualize something fresh. They make prose feel stale and, more important, if you read George Orwell's essay "Politics and the English Language," you'll see they're dangerous. Clichés, Orwell warns, think your thoughts for you.[†]

---

[*] Some people hate Strunk and White because they find it bossy. And others, like me, love that tiny book because it's short, useful, and just darned cute. There are plenty of guides that give similar advice. Just find one that speaks to you.

[†] Please google that essay immediately and read it at least twice. Don't get stuck on the first part where he gives hideous examples of academic prose. Skim the examples and get to his point.

You read over word packages and redundancies and don't even think about them as they come out of your mouth and spill onto the page. But if you spend a few seconds, you'll see why "final outcome," "first and foremost," "consensus of opinion," and "very unique" all have at least one needless word.

Most of us use junk phrases or wordy constructions. One that drives me nuts is starting a sentence with "Being that." I also can't stand "owing to the fact that" and "is the reason for" when you could just write *why* or *because*. Why write "I am able to" or "I am in a position to" when you mean "I can."

Vague words and linguistic fancification

I've told you words like *passionate*, *dedicated*, and *hardworking* are meaningless. Your job is to show, not tell. And by the way, leave *Webster's* out of it. Whenever someone writes, "If you look up the definition of 'perseverance' in the dictionary, you could find a description of me," a writing teacher loses her angel wings.

I've advised you to match the language in your materials with exactly what is on the job description; disregard this at your peril. Some of those words will be ugly but necessary. Some will be "zombie nouns." These, I happen to know, are called *nominalizations*—abstract ideas for which you get no mental picture. What does *intelligence* look like? How about *applicability*? How is an *investigation* conducted? What is an *investigation*? Does it look like library research? Or poking things in a laboratory with tweezers? Sherlock Holmes with his magnifying glass? A job ad for *Woofus* might require workers to conduct investigations into the owners of dogs who are known biters. In this case, you would be right to say you've "conducted investigations" into sociopathic cats and then describe how you counted the number of birds they killed and the devilish way they showed them off.

You want R2-D2 to light up. But if you're not matching words, you're better off losing multisyllabic vagueness like *investigation* and instead write you researched, or tracked, or dissected (um, maybe not that) evil felines.

Stick to language you would actually speak. Don't get all fancy. *Urinate* and *piss* mean exactly the same thing (though you probably don't want to use either in applying for jobs), and so do *fabricate* and *make*. If you made something, just say so. The extra syllables are not more technical or precise. You want to sound on the page the way you sound in real life.

Are rhetorical questions your friends?

Do you know how to make someone stop reading? Can you think of an annoying writing tic? Do you want someone to come up with reasons not to like you? Ask a rhetorical question. It will take readers away from the information you're trying to convey and get them to come up with their own answer.

Proofread, proofread, proofread

Spell check should be your best friend, but autocorrect can make you sound like a fool. Too many times in college admissions essays I saw this sentence: "That's why I want to attend Duke instead of a big pubic university."

So this next piece of advice is nonnegotiable: read everything you write out loud. Not in your head or under your breath, but loud enough that your dog leaves the room. Even better, have someone else read what you've come up with as you follow along. You'll hear where they stumble and where they run out of breath because your sentences don't have any commas and they just run on and on and by the time your reader gets to the period they will have to gulp air like water from a desert oasis that doesn't even exist and they will be very cross with you. You can also have Microsoft Word read your prose in one of four robotic voices. Do not skip this step. You will catch many, many mistakes. When I want to torture my students, I have them read their own work aloud in class. They cringe at slips they could easily have caught.

After a while, when you keep rereading what you've come up with, it starts to have the ring of inevitability. The words get stuck in your head and feel like they've been carved in stone. Not good. So I shift the way they look by changing the font. Nothing seems smart in Comic Sans. You'll find more infelicities of language if you can trick yourself into seeing your work anew, a re-vision.

Look, we all make mistakes in punctuation, often because the rules seem arbitrary. They are. In the United States periods and commas go inside quotation marks. In the United Kingdom it's the opposite. Americans use double quotes like "this" for everything except what's inside a quotation. Across the pond, it's as different as a Kit-Kat is from a Flake. Germans capitalize their nouns, but you'll look silly if you write "I am a great Team Player." Think of semicolons as loaded guns; they should be handled only by trained professionals. Exclamation points are needy and scream "Like me!"*

No one will ding you for getting that stuff wrong, though it's good to show you know the rules, especially if a job requires writing. Lots of typos and simple mistakes signal you're someone who doesn't pay attention to details. The real reason to follow the rules of grammar and syntax is simple: clarity.

---

*Yes, I've used some in this book because I want you to like me! Go ahead, call me needy.

Simple and direct is the way to go

I've gotten notes from people—physician's assistants, store managers, accountants—where I could not understand what they were trying to tell me. I mean, I literally couldn't get the message. You don't want the reader to have to call in a translator. Make your sentences simple and direct. If they get too long, break them into bite-size bits.

If you've paid attention, you'll see I've chosen not to do some of the things I'm advising here. I'm asking you to think about every sentence, and every word, and make sure it's what you want to say, then ask yourself if there's a better way.

Ignore these rules

Finally, here are some dumb rules you can ignore (that, to my surprise, are still being taught). You'll see I've broken every single one of them. If your teachers dinged you for any of these, take a photo of this page and send it to them as a passive-aggressive message. If they argue, give them my email (racheltoor@gmail) and I'll set them straight.

Never begin a sentence with *but* or *and*.
Never use contractions.
Never refer to the reader as you.
Never use the first-person pronoun I.
Never split an infinitive.
Never write a paragraph consisting of a single sentence.

No matter your goal—getting a job, earning a promotion, dating online—learning to write in clear, direct sentences that also give a sense of who you are will help you be successful.

**Some writing resources I like that are
as entertaining as they are useful**

Stephen King, *On Writing*
William Strunk and E. B. White, *The Elements of Style*
Patricia O'Conner, *Woe Is I*
Benjamin Dreyer, *Dreyer's English*
Mary Norris, *Between You and Me*
Ellen Jovin, *Rebel with a Clause*

And make sure you read George Orwell's essay, "Politics and the English Language" so you'll see what's at stake with bad writing (hint: the rise of totalitarianism).

Acknowledgments

Pre-COVID, whenever I visited my best friend Val in Chicago, I also made a point of having breakfast with Mary Laur, the editor of my previous book. When the pandemic grounded us all, Mary and I began having long chats on the phone.

We talked about work and life. I'd been stuck trying to write a book about a man I'd loved who died suddenly and, in a moment of frustration, I said, "Can you please come up with a project for us to do together that's fun and easier than sobbing on the page?"

She said, "Let me think about it and we can talk next week."

In the conversation that followed, she gave me an idea I thought was perfect—a project that would build on things I'd already done, play to my strengths, and allow me to develop a new set of skills.

"I'm in," I said.

"And I have another idea," she said.

That one was even better.

Mary told me that her friends in all kinds of industries complained about the job application materials young people submitted. Why not write a book to show them how to present themselves?

I tell this story because I love giving credit and thanks to Mary and because it illustrates much of what I've tried to tell you in this book. To recap:

I was stuck.

I asked someone who knows me for help.

She took stock of my talents and suggested something perfect, though not a project I would have thought up on my own.

I wasn't entirely qualified to do it but knew I could work hard to learn what I needed.

When I had difficulties along the way, I found people and resources to help.

Eventually I was able to achieve exactly what I'd hoped, and in a way that represented who I am. (Not exactly the "problems with kids today" she initially thought was needed but more "here's what I think might help you.")

Writing this book was intellectually stimulating and pure joy. I got to talk to a whole bunch of wonderful people and learned a ton along the way that I believe will be useful to others. Can you ask for anything more from work?

Now I get to thank the people who were kind enough to talk to me along the way, those who were in fact qualified to give advice from the hiring side.

Though I'm sure I'm missing some (like Carroll family members, all my other friends, and random strangers in hotel lobbies), the people whose advice and experiences were helpful to me are Larisa Abernethy, Ray Angle, Mike Bergmann, Nate Bryant, Jennifer Cast, Wenda Cenexant, Cheryl Chamberlain, Lisa Emtman, Tom Feulner, Ellyn Foltz, Matt Furst, Phil Gardner, Lynn Ann Gries, Steve Gump, Glenn Gutmacher, Tim Harding, Mikki Hubbard, Brandt Johnson, Ellen Jovin, Noah Leavitt, Heather Maietta, Max Mankin, Jay Manning, Sabrina Mauritz, Joy Peskin, Don Troop, Michael Watson, and Caitlin Wheeler.

And then there were the readers who weighed in with more advice: Taylor Brown, Valerie Chang, Lise Chapman, Martha Furst, Alex Holzman, Kasia Kalata, Michelle LaRoche, Nadia Mensah,

Tania Nunez-Guzman, Barb Protacio, Alex Richburg, Ellen Rome, Robin Schachter, Suzanne Wilson Summers, Caroline Woodwell, and Johan Zhang.

My gratitude goes to the anonymous peer reviewers for the University of Chicago Press who identified themselves after giving me final useful comments: Rebecca Taylor Brutus, Jamie Dunn, Keith M. Hearit, and Chris Mayer. Ellyn Foltz has been a source, a champion, and a trusted adviser from inception to final manuscript (and beyond).

Thanks to the editors who published bits of this while I was trying to tell faculty they need to make career readiness part of their teaching: Sarah Bray at *Inside Higher Ed* and Denise Magner at the *Chronicle of Higher Education*.

A number of Pro Tips came directly (sometimes in their language) from experts Michelle LaRoche and Robin Schachter; and for terrific feedback, including the idea to start the book with the fictional story of Olivia, I have to thank one of my best creative writing students ever, Tania Nunez-Guzman. Nadia Mensah provided a first stab at some of the Quick Takes.

I was lucky to have colleagues at Eastern Washington University who listened to me as I flapped in excitement about what I was learning, in particular Mindy Breen, Mary Voves, Nydia Martinez, and Angela Schwendiman. And students who served as guinea pigs for my strategies.

When I got to college, I was terrified of finding out that I'd been an admissions mistake. Even if that was true, Cindy Watts, Martha Furst, and Valerie Chang have made me feel like I belonged for the past four decades. If you get nothing else from college, I hope you come out with peeps like these.

My agent Elise Capron is an enduring fount of support, exclamation points, and shared dog mama doting.

At the Press, in addition to the editing, long conversations, and brownies provided by Mary Laur, I am grateful for the work of Jenni Fry, Beth Ina, Carrie Adams, and the editorial assistants in the Manuscript Editing Department. In the final stages of review, friends from various parts of life helped clean up my messes. Thanks to Margaret Waters, Kim Ribbens, Chad Massie, and John Paul.

Finally, I like to say that I won the pandemic.

At a time when so many were suffering, when the world closed down, my heart grew three sizes. Toby Carroll went from being someone I had a secret crush on (seemingly hopeless because he's younger, smarter, cooler, and kinder than I am) to becoming my partner—my person—and now, the co-parent of our dog, Harry. If I were to try to tell you how much I love those two guys, this book would be a thousand pages.

Being grateful is the best feeling in the world. And it should never go without saying.

Thanks, all.

Index

age discrimination, 50n*
AI. *See* artificial intelligence (AI)
Amazon, 56, 99, 137, 164
artificial intelligence (AI)
    bots, viii, 1, 2, 8, 39, 45, 46, 57–58,
      77, 86, 91–92, 112, 115, 128, 133,
      182
    and cover letters, viii, 91–92, 97
    and interviews, 133
    and resumes, 1, 8, 91, 112, 115
    and screening, viii, 60, 77, 86, 128,
      182
attitude, 17–26
    and character, 18
    of entitlement, 8, 77, 123, 156
    and experience, xi
    and hiring, 103
    and mindset, 14, 26
    quick takes, 26
    for rhetorical tasks, viii
authenticity, vii, 21, 81, 132–33, 153

Baby Boomers (generation), 53, 156
benefits and salaries. *See* salaries and
    benefits

capitalization, 107n*, 195
career centers and offices
    and automated tracking systems, 58
    and certifications, 72
    information, resources, and tools
      from, ix, ixn*, 29–31, 54, 55, 73
    and internships, 65
    and interview clothes, 135
    See also study groups
certifications, 5, 41, 69–72, 71n†, 77
    in cover letters, 89
character
    and attitude, 17–18
    and family responsibilities, 116
    traits, 18, 114
clichés
    in interviews, 146
    in writing, 91, 146, 192–93
coaching, 159–60
code-switching, x, 133
commitment, 63, 83, 86
    and resumes, 115, 118
contacts, 34–42
    collecting and documenting, 34n*,
      37–38, 50, 53, 55, 163
    and Google, 38–40
    and references, 170–72
    strangers as, 35–37, 41–42
    See also networking
cover letters, 85–111
    and artificial intelligence, viii, 91–
      92, 97

cover letters (*continued*)
  bad, xin*, 169
  checklist (practical pro tips), 110
  closures, 107–8
  and commitment, 86, 89
  contact information in, 108–10
  for conversations, 151
  drafts and versions, 97, 98
  and enthusiasm, 86, 89, 106
  and experience, 91, 103–6
  experience in, 91, 103–6
  first paragraphs of, 87–88
  formality in, 95, 110
  and humblebragging, 145
  and interests, 86
  and job requirements, 103–5
  key words to use in, 58, 60, 61–62,
    75, 89, 193
  length of (one page), 4, 58, 89, 96,
    110
  mistakes in, 100
  name in, 155
  as optional, not, 85–87, 110
  personality, conveying in, 187
  quantify in, 61n*
  quick takes, 110–11
  reading aloud, 108
  salutations, 92–96, 110
  second paragraphs of, 88–89
  sharing, 76
  sign-offs, 107–8
  simple formula for, 14, 92, 110
  storytelling in, 87–92, 99, 104–5,
    110
  submitting, 1, 90–91, 93
  tailored to job and organization,
    viii, 57–58, 77, 85, 91, 96–103,
    151, 183
  versions of, 98
  'Why now' paragraphs, xii, 105–7,
    110

"Why them," "Why me/you" para-
    graphs, 89, 98–103, 105, 110
  See also resumes
credibility, and fact-checking, 22n*
culture, workplace. *See* workplace
  culture
curiosity, 76
  and attitude, 21–23
  and eagerness, xii, 13, 49
  and enthusiasm, 21, 130
  and experience on resume, 118
  and humility, 49
  in interviews, 130, 150, 162
  and respect, xii, 150
  as thoughtful, 162

deadlines, 4, 28, 28n*, 30, 42n
  and follow up, 176
  and interviews, 146, 158
discrimination, x, 50n*, 58, 82–83, 157

eagerness, 16, 44, 68
  and attitude, 20–21
  and cover letters, 99, 101, 103, 106,
    111
  and curiosity, xii, 13, 49
  and follow up, 176, 178n*
  and humility, 49
  in interviews, 133, 152, 166
  and resumes, 119, 123
Elements of Style, The (Strunk and
    White), 114n*, 191–92, 192n*, 197
emails
  for application submission, 93
  checking regularly, 42–43, 42n*, 45,
    130, 166
  as contact information, 109–11
  for contacts, 37–38, 42–43
  for following up, 174–75
  good, 12n*
  for interview team, 174

for letter of recommendation, 94
phone numbers in, 109–11
professional-sounding address, 45
for professors, 13
and resumes, 127
time zones in, 109–11
emotional intelligence (EQ), 23
empathy, 2, 17, 88, 131–32, 145
enthusiasm, 15, 42, 46, 56, 183
  and attitude, 20–21
  and cover letters, 86, 89, 106
  and curiosity, 21, 130
  and excitement, 54, 106
  and follow up, 176
  in interviews, 129–30, 153
  and passion, 89
  and references, 171
  and veracity, 153
entitlement
  attitude of, 8, 77, 123, 156
  vs. privilege, 8, 123
EQ (emotional intelligence), 23
exaggerations, avoiding, 12, 71, 86,
  118–19
excitement
  for challenges and problems, 21,
    138
  and contributions, 100
  and dedication, 8
  and enthusiasm, 54, 106
  and following up, 176
  and gratitude, 176
  and honesty, 103
  and interviews, 131
  lack of, 137
experience, 3–4, 28, 45
  applicable, equivalent, related, or
    relevant, 4–5, 14–15, 16, 61, 65–
    69, 88, 101, 104–5, 110, 111, 113,
    115, 117, 120–21, 123–24, 143–44,
    151–52, 169, 181

and attitude, xi
and character traits, 114
in cover letters, 91, 103–6
equivalent, 67
and honesty, 151
and interviews, 163
in interviews, 132, 163
and job description, 58, 104–5
and passion, 65, 151
of peers, 35, 42, 54, 64, 75–77, 143
and professionalism, 7
and qualifications/requirements,
  5, 67–69
quantifying, 115, 191
"real world," 65–66
on resumes, 58, 112–18, 120–21,
  125
and skills, 19, 46, 63–64, 68, 87,
  98, 101, 113, 186
and training, 178
when following up, 176
See also internships; volunteering
extroverts, 18, 81
See also introverts

Facebook, 40–41, 41n*, 60, 68
fact-checking, 22n*, 118, 154
family responsibilities, and character, 116
fan mail, to authors of books you like,
  175
following up, 174–79
  emails for, 174–75
  and excitement, 176
  and interviews, 166
  manners matter, 174–76
  quick takes, 179
formality
  in cover letters, 95, 110
  and interviews, 135
  and politeness, 13, 54

formality (*continued*)
in resumes, 114
in writing, 13, 95, 95n†, 110, 114

Gen [Generation] X, 156
Gen [Generation] Z, 156
Glassdoor, and workplace culture, 64
Google
and contacts, 32, 34–36, 37–40, 83
and fact-checking, 118
and interview questions, 160
resources on, ix, 192n†, 197
for salary information, 176–77
GPA. *See* grade point average (GPA)
grade point average (GPA), 45
and attitude, 21
in cover letters, 86, 86n*
in interviews, 154
on resumes, 113, 119
grammar
and clarity, 195
mistakes in, avoiding, 4
and syntax, 195
and writing, 4, 139, 187–88, 188n*,
195
gratitude, 176, 202

hobbies, 5, 68, 81
on resumes, 113, 120–24, 128
homophobia, 40, 62
honesty, x
and attitude, 25
and authenticity, 132
in cover letters, 103
in interviews, 132, 151, 167
on resumes, 118, 128
humility, xii, 47–49, 184–85
and attitude, 17, 18–19, 24, 26
in cover letters, 93–94
and curiosity, 49
and deference, 94

and eagerness, 49
in interviews, 133, 145, 153

Indeed, job listings/postings, 97n*
internships, 5
in cover letters, 106
and experience, 28, 30–31, 45, 65–
66, 68, 72, 76
in interviews, 148
and references, 168
on resumes, 116, 118, 120
See also volunteering
interviews, 129–67
and artificial intelligence (AI), 133
and best version of yourself, 133,
166
clothing/dressing for, 30, 133, 134–
35, 148
and code-switching, 133
as conversations, 151
as discussions, 135n*
and following up, 166
and formality, 135
informational, 15, 34, 51–54, 64n*,
69, 107, 130–31, 182
and job descriptions, 131, 140, 142,
144, 151
listening during, 136, 166
mistakes during, 165–66, 167
and networking, 51
and note-taking, 132, 135n*, 145,
166, 179
practice and prepare for, 69, 162–
64, 167
procedures vary, 129–30
and professionalism, 7, 133, 135
questions, answering, 148
questions, to ask, 137–40, 158, 159–
62, 161n*, 166, 167
questions, to expect, 77, 137–39,
141–45, 153–54

quick takes, 166–67
recorded or video, 69, 129, 132–35, 145, 166
and respect, 150
and resumes, 127, 129, 131, 153–54
storytelling in, 140, 142
strengths and weaknesses addressed in, 139, 144, 145–48
and thank-you notes, 15, 56, 166, 174, 179
via telephone, 129–32, 134, 145
introverts, 17–18, 49–50, 81, 135n*
See also extroverts

job descriptions, 55–77
abbreviations in, 115
and aboutness of jobs, 74–75
and competencies, 18
decoding, 74–75
and experience, 58, 104–5
and interviews, 131, 140, 142, 144, 151
language and key words, 60, 61–62, 75, 86, 89, 113, 115, 128, 193–94
quick takes, 77
reading carefully, 88
and resumes, 2, 75, 89, 115
and skills, 5, 18
job fairs, 56, 136
job searches, 1–16, 27–54
and college admissions, x, 10–11, 12, 93, 145
and contact information, 45
deliberate and thoughtful, 81n*
documenting, ix, 34n*, 163
and effort, 183–85
and experience, 45
and feedback on process, 186
free advice, 56–58
and interests, 16, 84, 86, 184, 186
as job, 57

as long haul, 26, 180–86
and matches, x, 77, 78–84, 151–53
and matches, quick takes, xi, 83–84
and mindset, viii–ix, 9, 9n*, 12, 14, 25, 26, 92
as opportunity, 15, 16
and previous employees, asking about, 82, 84
questions to ask yourself, 80
quick takes, 16, 54, 186
as research project, 34n*, 64–65, 183
thoughtful and deliberate, 81n*
job titles, 44, 58–59

libraries and librarians, 72n*
and expertise, ix
jobs and careers in, 74, 86–87, 88, 114–15, 150
and online courses and certifications, 71–72
and research, 193
LinkedIn, 40–48, 50
activity section, 46–47
bots and algorithms, 44–47, 70
contact information on, 45
contacts on, 41–42, 45–46, 83, 170, 180
curated, 41n*
exploit for all it's worth, 54
free functions, 44
headshots, 30, 44, 126
job listings and postings on, 46, 93, 97n*
messages, 93, 109
name on, 44
networking on, 45–46
profiles, ixn*, 30, 42, 44–45, 70–71, 93, 100
resume on, 46
student accounts, 71–72

manners, when following up, 174–76
mentors and mentoring, 3, 6, 11, 67
   bosses as, 21, 59n*
   and contacts, 29, 36, 54
   and cover letters, 107
   and interviews, 140, 159–60
   and references, 171–72
   and resumes, 127
Microsoft, jobs at, 99
millennials (generation), 135, 156
mindset
   and attitude, 14, 26
   and contributions, 14
   fixed, 23, 138
   growth, 25, 138
   on the job, 18n*
   and job searches, viii–ix, 9, 9n*, 12,
      14, 25, 26, 92
   and point of view, 19
   of recruits, 20
   and skills, 16
   and team players, 26
mistakes
   and desperation, 9
   learning from, 17, 25, 103, 150, 166,
      178
   stupid, 14, 89n*
Mrs., avoid usage, 47n*, 95n‡

nerds, 33, 190–91, 191n*
networking, 31–35
   and building relationships, 42
   and connectors, 32–33
   and contacting strangers, 35–37, 54
   continuous and ongoing, 183
   as essential, 75
   and Google, 38–40
   and interviews, 51
   and job openings, 55
   on LinkedIn, 45–46
   with peers, 75–77
   in person, 54

and resources, 55
   See also contacts

phone calls, 53, 54, 68
   in cover letters, 108–11
   and interviews, 130–32, 134, 166
   and time zones, 109–11
   See also voicemail
politeness
   and formality, 13, 54
   and professionalism, 47, 56
privilege, ixn*, x, 5, 152–53
   vs. entitlement, 8, 123
professionalism, 37, 82
   and experience, 7
   and interviews, 7, 133, 135
   and personalizing, viin*, 100
   and politeness, 47, 56
proofreading, 4, 71, 129, 134–35
   and writing tricks, 189, 194–95
punctuation
   and writing, 4, 195

qualifications, 5
   and cover letters, 85, 91, 101, 103–5,
      111
   and interviews, 140, 142–43, 161
   in job descriptions, 59–62, 67–69
   and job matches, 78, 83
   and responsibilities, 59–62
   and resumes, 125
questions
   to ask yourself, 80
   and listening, 21
   rhetorical, 194
   smart, 24
   stupid, 24, 50, 76n*
Quick Takes, 14
   attitude, 26
   cover letters, 110–11
   following up, 179
   interviews, 166–67

job descriptions, 77
job searches, 16, 54, 83–84, 186
job searches, and matches, 83–84
references, 172–73
resumes, 128

racism, 40, 62
recruiting, as job, 56
references, 168–73
   asking for, 168–72
   and contacts, 170–72
   and good relationships, 173
   personal, 173
   quick takes, 172–73
   relevant, 168, 171
   separate from resumes, 4, 168
requirements. See qualifications
resumes, 112–28
   acronyms and jargon on, 126
   and artificial intelligence (AI), 1, 8,
      112, 115
   contact information on, 109
   for conversations, 151
   customized and tailored to job and
      organization, viii, 46, 57–58, 77,
      85, 91, 115, 127, 128, 151, 183
   and emails, 127
   and experience, 58, 112–18, 120–
      21, 125
   formality in, 114
   gaps, 119–20
   generic on LinkedIn, 46
   and interviews, 127, 129, 131, 153–54
   and job descriptions, 2, 75, 89, 115
   key words to use in, 2, 58, 60, 61–
      62, 75, 89, 115, 128, 193
   length of (one page), 4, 58, 89, 128
   name on, 44, 155
   padding, avoid, 125n*
   personality, conveying on, 187
   quantities and numbers on, 61n*,
      113, 115, 128, 191–92

questions about, 153–54
quick takes, 128
scanned and screened, 8, 68, 87
sharing, 76
skills on, 71
storytelling on, 128
submitting, 1, 51, 56, 93, 127, 128,
   131, 170, 182
versions of, 113, 127
what not to include, 125–26
in Word format, 112–13
See also cover letters

salaries and benefits, 46, 183
   and follow up, 176–79
   and interviews, 159, 165
   and job descriptions, 72–73, 73n*
sexism, 40, 62
skills
   and accomplishments, 45
   and competencies, 18
   and experience, 19, 46, 63–64, 68,
      87, 98, 101, 113, 186
   and mindset, 16
   on resumes, 71
   without college degrees, 11n*
social media
   checks of self, 39
   embarrassing and ill-considered,
      viii, 39
   as job, 60
   and privacy, viii, 39–40, 54
   as tasteful, 54
spelling
   and writing, 3, 4, 170, 194
storytelling
   in application materials, vii
   in cover letters, 87–92, 95n*, 99,
      104–5, 110
   in interviews, 140, 142
   on resumes, 128
   and success, 142

Strunk, William, 114n*, 191–92, 192n*, 197
study groups, 76, 108, 149
  See also career centers and offices
stupid mistakes, repeated, 14, 89n*
stupid questions, 24, 50, 76n*

teachable moments, 48n*
team players, 18, 26, 80, 150
teleology, 51, 51n*
telephone calls, 53, 54, 68
  in cover letters, 108–11, 109–11
  and interviews, 130–32, 134, 166
  and time zones, 109–11
  See also voicemail
thank-you notes, 15, 56
  and follow up, 174, 179
  and interviews, 166
TikTok, 61, 127, 161
Toor, Rachel, xn*, 187
totalitarianism, and bad writing, 197
training, new job, 178
Twitter (now X), 40

values
  of companies and organizations, 6,
    62–65, 80, 83, 87–88, 151
  personal, 6, 12, 15, 63, 79–81, 83, 88,
    156, 181
voicemail
  and cover letters, 109, 111
  as first impression, 53
  and interviews, 130
  semiformal, 54
  See also phone calls
volunteering
  and experience, 45, 65–67
  on resumes, 113–14, 116–17, 120,
    122
  See also internships
vulnerabilities, 145

well-being, 63
White, E. B., 114n*, 191–92, 192n*, 197
word clouds, 75
work experience. *See* experience
workplace culture, ix, 50–51, 182
  and attitude, 24
  and cover letters, 99, 105–7
  and follow up, 177
  and interviews, 135–36, 156, 159n*
  and job descriptions, 59, 62–65, 69,
    74–75, 77
  and job matches, 78–80, 82–83
  and resumes, 124
*Write Your Way In: Advice on Crafting
  an Unforgettable College Admissions Essay* (Toor), xn*, 187
writing
  academic prose, 192n†
  and action verbs, 126
  and adverbs, 192
  agency and action in, 191
  bad, 197
  and brevity, 190
  and capitalization, 107n*, 195
  and clarity, 190, 195
  clichés in, 91, 146, 192–93
  concise, 187, 188
  as conversational, vii, viin*, 44
  direct and simple, 196
  and fan mail to authors of books
    you like, 175
  first drafts, viii, 90–91, 90n*, 97,
    102, 142, 189
  in first person, xn*, 187
  formality in, 13, 95, 95n†, 110, 114
  good, viin*, 86–87, 98, 124, 192
  and grammar, 4, 139, 187–88,
    188n*, 195
  -*ing*, usage, 189
  it, usage, 191
  Microsoft reading of, 195

mistakes, avoiding, 4, 195
personality in, viin*, 187
and prepositions, 190
proofreading, 4, 71, 129, 134–35,
    189, 194–95
and punctuation, 4, 195
quantify, vs. qualify, 191–92
reading aloud, 195
repetition, avoiding, ix
resources, 197
rules, 196
and self-understanding, 90
simple and direct, 196
as skill, 97–98
specific and vivid, 97, 124, 192
and spelling, 3, 4, 170, 194
and success, 191n*
and thinking, viiin*, 14n†
this, that, and there, usage, 189–91

tricks, xn*, 14, 187–97
typos, avoiding, 195
vague words and linguistic fancifi-
    cation, avoiding, 193–94
verbs, action, 126
verbs, strong, 192
vivid and specific, 97, 124, 192
and word clouds, 75
See also storytelling

X (formerly known as Twitter), 40

Yelp, 69

Zoom
and contacts, 49–50, 52–53, 53n*,
    69, 72
and headshots, 44
for interviews, 132, 134